THE COURAGE TO DEAL WITH DIFFICULT PEOPLE *INCLUDING YOURSELF*

BY BETTY PERKINS, MS

TZEDAKAH PUBLICATIONS
Sacramento, California

For information, address
Tzedakah Publications
P.O. Box 221097
Sacramento, CA 95822

Cover illustration by Heather Cooper.
Cover design by Mary Burroughs, Creative Director of
Comstock's Design & Litho and Diane Sutherland Art Direction.
Inside text design by Mary Burroughs, Creative Director,
Kristen Rasmussen and Jill Raymond of Comstock's Design & Litho.

Library of Congress Cataloging-in-Publication Data
Perkins, Betty, 1943-
Lion Taming: the courage to deal with difficult
people, including yourself / by Betty Perkins. — 1st edition
p. cm.
Includes bibliographical references.
ISBN 0-929999-10-x: $14.95
Psychology / Self-Help
1. Interpersonal conflict.   2. Fear–Psychological aspects.
3. Interpersonal relations.   I. Title.
BF637.I48P47 1995   94-48408
158'.2–dc20   CIP

10 9 8 7 6 5 4 3 2 1

TABLE OF CONTENTS

*This book is dedicated to
my husband, Michael,
whose unflagging love and belief
in me nourishes my soul.*

If we could read the secret history of our enemies, we should find in each man's life sorrow and suffering enough to disarm all hostility.

⤛ Henry Wadsworth Longfellow ⤜
"Driftwood"

FOREWORD

*D*ifficult people are the weed and feed for your internal state. I began studying the topic after landing a job, then perceiving myself six months later as a source of annoyance to a colleague. Wanting to avoid conflict and be valued for my contributions, I alternated between placating behavior and blaming. At the time, I didn't know that my goals—to get this person to like me, work easily with me, and be glad that I was there—were impossible ones. I didn't understand then that I don't need anyone other than myself to change for my life to be happy, productive, excellent. I didn't understand then that what was upsetting me was not the person I perceived as difficult but my own unacknowledged fear, which I saw reflected back by that individual.

I scoured bookstores and libraries for information that might give me the magical key to extricate myself from a situation that grew worse each month. Jerry Jampolsky's book **Love Is Letting Go of Fear** led me to **A Course in Miracles**, a set of three books containing a self-taught spiritual psychotherapy. Both conveyed the same message: I am never upset for the reason I think. I discovered the upset feeling that convinced me I was being victimized by a difficult person was separate from the actual conflict. That understanding is the foundation of this book.

After three years of gathering effective techniques from books and actively working on myself, I felt a new freedom. I knew that there was no such thing as failure, only feedback. The turning point for me occurred one day at work when a man in the middle *of a meeting suddenly and unexpectedly became hostile. Instead of feeling my familiar fear response, I felt eager: "Oh, boy!" I thought. "A chance to do some valuable research!" Armed with a variety of ways to respond to a difficult person, I faced each conflict with confidence. More and more, these interactions brought peace. When they did not—when my approach increased the other person's fear and the conflict escalated—I simply welcomed that feedback and switched to a different strategy or a different technique until I found one that worked.*

This book represents more than ten years of research distilled into the most potent strategies. As you read it, I will ask you to acknowledge the power of your thoughts and intuition. I will encourage you to stretch your comfort zone so that you can stand comfortably in the presence of your own and other people's fear and its manifestations: anger, jealousy, frustration, hatred, envy, anxiety, hopelessness. You will learn how you can remove those negative opinions in your mind that freeze a person in the "difficult" role. I will teach you how to recognize and own your own "stuff"—that physical response in your body that signals that you are stressed. This ability not only prevents a volatile or stressful situation from becoming worse, but also gives you direction about sensitive areas in your life that need to be addressed, such as aspects of yourself you have denied, childhood wounds, unexpressed anger, and unshed grief. You will learn various methods to heal your "stuff," using simple techniques described in this book, such as seeking more satisfying employment and accepting death in your life. Out of this fertile soil of introspection and the introduction of interpersonal communication techniques will grow your ability to be someone who can successfully interact with people who are considered difficult.

The examples in this book are taken from my workshops and classes, my own experiences, and conversations with employees who have allowed me to coach them. Names have been changed for privacy.

I have many people to thank for their contributions to this project. First, my appreciation to the people who helped me to produce this book: To David Cawthorn, publisher and number one fan throughout the project, who allowed me the freedom to swear at him on paper when I was frustrated. Thank you to Jim Merk for his valuable editing and infinite patience. To Heather Cooper, whose beautiful painting adorns the front cover of this book. Thank you to Mary Weddle and Ruth Letner for their feedback. Thank you to Carlie, my golden retriever, who was less than three feet away whenever I wrote at home and who knew when to signal that it was time to play. To Java City coffee shops, where my writing was inspired by delicious cappuccinos and lattés. Thank you to the staff at Marine World Africa USA in Vallejo, California, and the Sacramento Zoo for their information about the nature of African lions.

I am grateful to the significant people in my life who love and encourage me: my children, Mishel and Chelsea, who gave me the gift of turning out well; my parents, who taught me how to enjoy my life and to be true to myself; my siblings—Judy Wells, Stan Wells, and Wendy Palmer—who are all dear friends; and Stan's and Wendy's significant partners, Christy and Don. To my niece, Tracy, and her husband, Doug, for providing a writing chair, and to my nephew, Greg; his wife, Laurie; and their children. And to my mother- and father-in-law, who are not difficult people.

I am also grateful for the presence of friends in my life who cheered me on: my buddy Anne Evans, Bob Sellers for his humor and his training in Imaginal Therapy, Judy Svoboda, Linda Clark, Sherry Lynn, Andrea Kelly, and Tracy Murphy; Bob Shreve and Kitty McMahon; Alice and Gunnar Vestergaard; and Jerry and Kerri Walker. To my secretary, Sarah Pacquette, and to my friends at work, Greg Anderson, Sandra Dussault, Hal Eilersen, Annette Johnson, Susan Northart, and Marilee Sullivan. To the entire staff of Gibbons San Juan Psychological Services and to the White House Counseling Center. My thanks to Terri Drake Sellers, who showed me that it's OK to die. Thank you to band members Steve and Anne Evans, Mike Perkins, Stan Wells, Tony Paglione, and Mark McPhail and to music in my life.

Thank you to the San Juan Unified School District, especially Mike Parks, and to the Auburn Union High School District, both who hired me and provided me with my own educational experiences with difficult people. Thank you to those authors and other sources of education, including Jerry Jampolsky, Peter McWilliams, Marianne Williamson, Wayne Dyer, Deepak Chopra, the text, workbook, and teacher's manual for A Course in Miracles; and the Sacramento Attitudinal Healing Center. Thank you to my former husband, Tom, who feared that much of this book would be about him, and his wife, Brenda, for their help in raising our children. Thank you to Dr. Maria Nemeth, who encouraged me to set the goal of writing the book in her "You and Money" course and who told her publisher to call me. Finally, thank you to all the teachers who came into my life disguised as difficult people.

INTRODUCTION

*A*re you someone who thinks you have done something wrong when the person you are dealing with is angry? Who tries to get people to like you? Who gets a queasy feeling when given criticism? Who yells or blames others when you are angry to get relief and obtain results? Who is in a relationship with someone whom you believe is a difficult person? Who believes how you feel is determined by how others treat you? Who becomes uncomfortable in the presence of tears or anger? If so, then this book is for you. It will show you how people you perceive as difficult can accelerate your inner growth. They do so by functioning as a mirror by reflecting back the denial, resentment, guilt, judgment, and blame in yourself—getting right to the source of your own buried pain and fear.

The lions referred to in the title of this book are those who trigger a feeling in you that is anything other than well-being. A lion can be a hostile person, someone who withdraws from you, someone who is critical, or someone who is a chronic complainer. It can be a stranger, spouse, relative, co-worker, child, friend, or neighbor. A lion can be a grocery clerk, police officer, therapist, or telemarketer. In short, lions can be anyone. Lion taming, then, is dealing with these people in positive ways and improving these relationships. It is acknowledging the choice you have between feeding the fear underlying the difficulty or defusing it. It is acting with dignity and respect, even in situations that may appear to be out of control.

This book will encourage you to venture out and help you to see difficult people differently. In the chapters that follow, you will learn methods to change your relationship with difficult people as you build courage. By developing these skills, you will increase both your efficiency and your enjoyment in the workplace. Being able to get along well with people is one of the most valuable commodities in getting a job, keeping a job, and earning promotions. In your family, you can provide leadership for increased intimacy and well-being. With your friends, you will be able to express your real self safely. In your other significant relationships, you will be able to handle conflict as it comes up in a way that empowers everyone involved.

In Chapter 1, "The Invisible Realm," you will learn about the invisible force that unites us all and that provides strength and energy to those who wish to tap into it, and you will learn about the power of our thoughts, which shape our reality and have a far greater impact on our relationships than you might first assume. This chapter also reminds you to listen to your inner voice, that gentle source of wisdom within yourself that can be heard best in moments of silence.

Chapter 2, "The Comfort Zone," focuses on that safe area where we hide, unchallenged and unlikely to grow. If fear stops you from taking risks with difficult people—that is, if you rely on placating or blaming, as many do—you will not be as effective in dealing with them as you would be otherwise. This chapter will empower you to stretch your comfort zone and take control of your fear.

In Chapter 3, "Removing the Mask of the Lion," you will learn how to remove negative characterizations of yourself and others, freeing yourself and those you interact with of the judgments that hinder open communication.

In Chapter 4, "Meeting the Inner Lion," you will learn how to reach your ideal state in any circumstance by recognizing your "stuff"—that physical reaction you get in your body when you are under stress—and learning how to separate it from the situation you are in.

Chapter 5, "Healing the Inner Lion," outlines a process for healing your "stuff" that includes shedding swallowed tears, delivering undelivered communications, expressing anger and other negative feelings responsibly, and owning all aspects of yourself.

To further heal your "stuff," Chapter 6, "Satisfying the Inner Lion," addresses the importance of bringing meaning and integrity into your life.

In Chapter 7, "Tools of the Trade," you will learn ways of responding to anger other than submitting or attacking, placating or blaming. You will learn responses to verbal aggression that maintain your dignity while defusing the abuser, and create unconscious rapport even while you are under attack.

Chapter 8, "Death: The Invisible Ringmaster," invites you to consider bringing an acceptance of death into your life. Behind difficult relationships lies fear, and the greatest and generally the most unacknowledged fear is the fear of death. By welcoming death into your life, you free yourself of its power over you.

At the end of each chapter, you will find exercises that give you the opportunity to practice the skills I've introduced. I hope you will take the time to do them as you complete each chapter, allowing a day or two to practice each of them. You may wish to purchase a notebook before you begin reading. Writing down your experiences as you experiment not only helps you to integrate the material into your life but will provide a helpful record of your progress (some people find bringing peace into their lives so natural a process that they need the journal to document the progress that otherwise would go unnoticed).

Take a few moments to consider making the following commitments to yourself. Over the next thirty days, are you willing to:

- ❧ Go the extra mile with one person, taking all the time required to produce a positive result?
- ❧ Experiment with your state of fear when you meet a difficult person?
- ❧ Stop trying to change people?
- ❧ Examine the disowned parts you project onto others?

If you answered "no" to any of these questions, thank you for your honesty. Mark a time in your calendar when you are willing to reconsider making these commitments.

If you answered "yes" to these questions, you are ready to enter the arena. Welcome! As you gain skill and come to understand that people are either in a state of love or in a state of fear (and asking for help), you will feel increasingly secure in situations that previously sent you reeling. You will be able to take a stand and deliver your truth as a peaceful warrior. Do not underestimate the importance of this step. By improving your relationship with the difficult people around you, you will improve the world because what you do affects not only the people in your life but the people in their lives, multiplying outward, creating a growing community based on peace and understanding.

1

THE INVISIBLE REALM

What is essential is invisible to the eye.

—Antoine de Saint Exupéry, *The Little Prince*

Breath is the junction point between mind, body, and spirit. Every change of mental state is reflected in the breath and then in the body.

—Deepak Chopra, M.D., *Ageless Body, Timeless Mind: A Quantum Alternative to Growing Old*

Some people daydream about all sorts of unpleasant things. They rehearse imaginary quarrels, imaginary injustices, accidents, misfortunes, and because they do believe that such things could happen, and because thought is creative, they actually bring them upon themselves.

—Emmet Fox, *Around the Year with Emmet Fox*

The lion tamer who steps into the arena to face wild animals carries with her the tools of her profession and the skills she has honed through many hours of preparation. In addition to these, she brings one other important resource: her ability to tap into the invisible realm of energy, imagination, and intuition. In some respects, this is her most important resource because the more developed it is, the greater her confidence and her ability to hone her skills and to be flexible in times of pressure. And just as physical ability can be improved through training and practice, so can she, by practicing trust in herself, learn to develop her powers in these areas.

In the following chapters, you will learn to expand your comfort zone, recognize and remove your characterizations, acknowledge and heal what I call your "stuff," and much more. First, though, I want to introduce you to the invisible realm—a boundless source of energy and knowledge that often goes unacknowledged. I'm speaking not only of the amazing life force called ki by the Japanese, but of your mind and your intuition, that wise but often ignored inner voice that I call your Intuitive Knower. By "mind," I don't mean your intellectual ability. I'm referring to your ability to visualize your success in dealing with difficult people and, even more important, your ability to choose your own perceptions. Despite what most of us believe, our thoughts and emotions are very much in our control, and the person who understands the connection between her mind and her perception is in a very powerful position. The techniques for dealing with difficult people that I will describe in Chapter 7 are powerful, but their impact is even greater when they are power charged by ki, your mind, and your trust in your Intuitive Knower.

Electricity for the Soul

I want to share with you something I have learned about a remarkable source of energy and information. I think of it as electricity for the soul. Like electricity, it is an invisible source of power—in this case, power in the form of energy, strength, and wisdom. Unlike electricity, though, this source is available to us anytime and anywhere, and those "electrical engineers" among us working with this power need not fear painful electrocution because tapping into this energy brings only good. If you truly understand electricity and the circuits you're working with, you always will be able to make the connection, and you will bring about amazing things. If you are an amateur and you don't fully understand the principles involved, you may spend a lifetime of frustration trying to make that connection—like trying to relate effectively to a difficult person without knowing how. When you understand the principles of tapping into this source, though, you become like the electrical engineer who can work his magic in practically any situation and bring light and warmth where once there was darkness and cold.

With electrical engineers, the task is getting the electricity to do something useful. With you and me, the task is getting the source of power to connect between us and the difficult person. How do we make the connection?

Tapping the Invisible Power

The invisible power available to you in an interaction with a difficult person is demonstrated through aikido, a Japanese art of self-defense. Aikido means "the way of blending energy."[1] I am not a martial artist, but I trained in aikido long enough to understand the concept of ki (in Chinese, it's chi), which translates into "energy," "life force," or "vital essence." Seen through the eyes of one trained in aikido, an attacker is accepted as he is, and the "attackee" blends his energy with the opponent's force and momentum and moves out of the way. Being flexible enough to change with the attacker is a key in aikido. The ki, which originates from the lower area of the abdomen called the solar plexus, is available to all of us. Breathing and control of the ki develop after one has mastered some of the basic moves in aikido. The process of using ki to create a ball of energy that can be used to improve a difficult situation is described below in a woman's story of her success in brightening up a dull sermon.

Shortly after my introduction to aikido, I saw the benefit of introducing the idea of ki to my students. I have used the following "energy arm" exercise[2] with graduate students and continuation high school students sporting tough guy facades. With a partner, have the subject extend one arm straight out and have the partner try to bend the arm while the subject resists by using muscle. In this instance, the subject strains, holding his arm extended using muscle and force. Next, the same subject extends his arm straight out as before, this time visualizing that his arm is a hose with water spraying full force through his relaxed but extended arm, his fingers (representing the spray of water from the nozzle) waving easily. Remarkably, everyone is able to succeed at this wonderful exercise.

Students who participate in this exercise discover that they can gain access to an even greater power than they would using muscle and might. From this exercise, the students experience the invisible power of their ki through visualization. They replace tension and struggle with relaxation and peace, while they maintain an even greater vitality and strength than mere muscle alone could bring. What I think is most important about this demonstration is that it allows us to see that we can be more effective using peace when dealing with difficult people (and in all aspects of our lives) rather than using brute force or anger.

I was struck with the similarity between how aikido experts connect with their opponent without unnecessary force and the methods I had been using to connect with a difficult person. I had been using all the techniques that I describe later in this book: removing my characterization, visualizing the person surrounded by clear light, remembering that what I was observing was the person's fear, and imagining the person without the fear. I further imagined the two of us having an ideal conversation. By silently connecting in my imagination with the person being difficult, what began in my mind eventually became a reality with the person. What started as a visualization of clear light surrounding us both, including us in its warm glow, became an actual connection of trust between two people solving a problem.

While I was enrolled in aikido, I started to practice extending my ki at odd times: during meetings; at a conference when I was having trouble concentrating; or when working with a difficult student, teacher, or parent. The result was a connection with the person on whom I focused. The experience of accessing one's ki is one of powerful peace. The other person feels the connection, too. One woman in a workshop, after practicing Exercise 1 at the end of this chapter, wrote in her journal:

> While visiting my parents in another state, I attended church services with them. The sermon was extremely long and preachy. Sitting in a pew in the third row, I found myself bored and began negatively judging the minister. I switched my attention to my solar plexus and imagined myself becoming surrounded by a beautiful white light. I then extended the ball of light, imagining it was big enough to include the preacher. As I did this, I felt peaceful and full of love. It was a wonderful feeling for me, better by far than the bored, judging state I had been creating. At the end of the service, the man came over to me and said, "I felt a real connection to you. I don't know what to say about it except I felt you were really with me." My parents looked at each other and exclaimed, "What a kook!"

To aikido masters, a conflict is not judged as right or wrong. Instead, it is seen as energy. The warrior blends his energy with his opponent's energy. By going with the momentum and force of the opponent's energy, he is guided gently but powerfully in that same direction, leading the attacker to fall off balance. If you remove your concept that "so-and-so is being difficult" and accept the situation as it is, you don't need to use up so much energy. What if there were no such thing as the idea of a person being difficult? What if when someone was in a state of fear manifesting as anger, the most important thing another could do is be with that person until the anger ran down?

The Power of Thought

One of the most important aspects of learning to deal with difficult people (and, in a greater sense, in taking control of your life) is acknowledging that what we choose to think about determines how we feel, and how we feel in turn influences what choices we make. It is a fairly simple concept, but many of us have difficulty accepting it.

In his book *Feeling Good*, David Burns, M.D., talks about the relationship between a person's thinking process and his moods. When negative thought patterns are reversed, the physical symptoms of depression are alleviated. The startling results obtained from cognitive behavior therapy alone are attributable to the power of thought. Clinically depressed patients who changed their automatic negative thought patterns relieved their own depression at a much higher rate than patients put on a regimen of medication alone.[3] In other words, even if you suffer from depression, your thoughts, not external events or your physiology alone, play an important role in creating your moods.

In addition to choosing your thoughts, you choose the general attitude with which you go through your life. The choice you make about what your attitude will be in any situation determines whether you experience yourself as a helpless victim at the mercy of external events or as an active participant in the co-creation of your life. Even in the most dire circumstances, one's choice of attitude can create bright spots, as we see in the example below.

In *Man's Search for Meaning*, Holocaust survivor Viktor Frankl writes about suffering interspersed with idyllic moments spent thinking of his beloved wife or roasting pilfered potatoes. In his preface to Frankl's moving book, Gordon W. Allport writes:

> In the concentration camp every circumstance conspires to make the prisoner lose his hold. All the familiar goals in life are snatched away. What alone remains is the last of human freedoms—the ability to choose one's attitude in a given set of circumstances.[4]

Frankl (whose father would give him his own food rations in the camps, telling his son, "I'm not hungry") attributes performing acts of kindness to friends and family as the way to choose a life of meaning and peace even in the worst of settings. Can you imagine being taken from your life and all your belongings? Being forced to live without adequate clothing, food, cleanliness, and dignity? Seeing your loved ones extinguished and then still finding meaning and moments of peace in your life?

What is the nature of your attitude? Do you focus on the negative, or do you seek the positive and work to build on it? Do you tend to blame others for the condition of your moods rather than accept responsibility for your choices? Do you view people in your life whom you think are being difficult as wrong? Your upset is the product of your thoughts, not that other person.

Visualization

One aspect of our thinking is particularly helpful in overcoming difficulty with others, and that is visualization. Some class participants claim they can't visualize, and, they shut down if I use the word in an exercise. Actually, we all visualize even though we are not always aware of it. I'm using the term visualization to mean thinking about something with pictures, words, and feelings. When you visualize, you are either remembering something from the past or creating a future scene in your mind. There are varying degrees of how these images appear, from picture perfect as if watching a movie, to a vague memory or impression of something. When you think about something, your brain does many things: There is conversation (that is, you are either saying things out loud or thinking them silently), and there is imaging (as when you remember scenes from the past or create new ones that might occur in the future), and through these processes, you create feelings in your body. Then what follows—how you act and what occurs—is what you make of it all. When you are thinking, you are creating. You create how you feel and thus affect your action afterward.

How you go through your life is determined largely by the pattern of your thought process. Now, consider a few different kinds of examples. I've divided them into what appears to be "automatic" visualization (that is, those thoughts that appear to overtake us) and deliberate visualization (that is, those we are more aware of choosing). Both are, in fact, choices; one is simply more delayed than the other.

"Automatic"

- You see an advertisement that shows someone biting into your favorite kind of chocolate candy bar. You begin to make images in your mind of that candy bar, of unwrapping it, biting into it, and tasting its wonderful flavor. Your mouth waters. As you imagine this experience, you feel good, and later in the day, you can't get the image out of your head, and you find yourself at a market buying one.
- You make a mistake. Off and on all day long, you think of your mistake, imagining the worst consequence that could happen as a result of your error, and you get a certain feeling in your body. This feeling reminds you of other mistakes that you have made. You remember them; they return to you in images, conversation, and feelings associated with these other errors from the past. You decide you are incompetent.
- Someone blames you angrily for something you haven't done. You feel hurt and angry, and you want to defend yourself. You remember other acts of hostility by the person. You decide that you won't be able to get along with the person in the future.
- You hear a catchy song on the radio that you dislike and then can't seem to get it out of your head.

Deliberate

- You read a menu while sitting in a restaurant and imagine how several of the listed items will taste before you order.
- You look at an article of clothing and imagine how you would look in it or how the material would feel on your skin.
- You intend to write a letter, and you think about what

you will say. You imagine the face of the person you will write to, and in your mind you review events from your past, choosing which ones to describe in the letter.

❧ After thinking about that candy bar from the earlier example, you see yourself with another inch on your hips, visualize yourself taking a walk instead, and decide against buying the candy bar. In both cases, what you visualized determined your behavior.

In the example that follows, a situation of what appears to be an "automatic" visualization becomes a chosen one. A woman wrote in her journal that she was burned out because of downsizing in her company, and the prospect of spending another twenty years in her current job was depressing to her:

> *My company went from 2,000 employees to 800. Each of us is doing the work of two or more people now. I come home completely exhausted every evening, between seven and seven-thirty. My kids spend more time with the babysitter than with me. I miss their important school events like plays and parent conferences because of work. I can't take my vacation time because there's too much to do. On the weekends, in addition to doing the chores that need to be done, I do work that must be completed before Monday. My house is a mess all the time. We don't eat well because there's no time for grocery shopping. But I can't leave my job. There is so much competition out there that any twenty people would trade places with me in a minute. I wouldn't be able to find other employment.*

Do you become depressed with her as you read this passage? Do you empathize with her and remember news articles that validate her bleak perception of employment opportunities? After reading this passage, do you worry about the job outlook for yourself, your children, or others you care about? When she told her story in class, many others who were in similar situations bought into the hopelessness of her story of being stuck where she was, as if there were no other way, and felt pity for her. We allow these stories to increase our fears about the state of the world and our lives. Reports by the media help to fuel these fears as we bathe ourselves in stories each day of the crucial events of the world: grim statistics about job opportunities and disturbing tales of homelessness and crime. We create a distorted, rather than realistic, perception of the world and ourselves in it. Then, rather than imagining ourselves as one of the thousands who are happily employed, we assume the worst for ourselves.

In class, this woman took her journal entry and responded to it by thinking of its opposite; that is, she wrote down and then visualized her best-case scenario at the beginning and end of each day. She was excited by the possibility of creating ease in her life. The journal entry that follows tells of the changes she made within a month, simply by stopping her thoughts that she was stuck:

> *Since I felt my life was out of control, I took a week of vacation to determine what I would do about it. That decision alone provided some relief, because I knew I was not going to continue with my life as it was. The weekend before my vacation, I hired a student to clean my house for the day and went with my son to play all day. We went to the zoo, had a picnic lunch, then saw a movie. When we got home, the house was spotless, all the laundry washed, the scent of furniture polish in the air. "What's that smell?" my son asked, and I told him that it was the smell of our lives being in balance. When I put him to bed that night, I read him the story "The Red Shoes." It reminded me of my own life, which had run away with me. I had traded my life and my son's life for a paycheck.*
>
> *The next morning, a Sunday, I fixed pancakes for the two of us, and while my son played nearby with his cars, I read the Help Wanted section of the newspaper, underlining any job that appealed to me at all. Oddly enough, after doing this, I felt better about my job. I noticed that what appealed to me I already had. So I decided, instead of changing my job, I would change how I thought about it. Whereas before I would try to*

keep up with others who were working until past seven, I worked until five. Occasionally I would accommodate the work load by going in early or staying late. But I stopped making a habit of working overtime since I had found previously that after a while, what you do in an emergency becomes what is expected on a daily basis. I arranged to use a modem so I could work two days a week from my home. By working at home part of the time and getting my life more in balance, my productivity increased by twenty-five percent!

You visualize all the time. When you take time—even for a short period, such as a minute or two at the end of your negative "automatic" thoughts—to create a deliberate visualization, you powerfully affect your present and your future.

Finding the Stillness

When your "automatic" thoughts create stress in your body, it is beneficial to clear yourself of those feelings. Your breath is your pathway to finding stillness inside even when others around you are churning up with stress. Breathing is the built-in mechanism for being able to slow down a habit that seems automatic—for example, repeating negative thought patterns—and then change it or add on to it. When the tendency is to tense up in an interaction with a difficult person, withdraw because of fear, or speed up your conversation, the breath will be your key to intervention. Your breath will allow you to pause and listen for guidance, to sort through and past your "automatic" thoughts.

Pauses need to be inserted between your thoughts, especially when you are under stress. Otherwise, they will barrel along crazily like an out-of-control vehicle. I find a parallel in music. Music is a vital part of my life. It feeds my soul in a way that nothing else can. When I play music with one of the bands I belong to, I feel euphoric and unconcerned about what others think. At band practice, when we play a song too fast, putting in the wrong beats, it sounds horrible and we all laugh. The music from our songs comes not only from the notes, but from the spaces between the notes. A continuous stream of notes hurts the ears. One note played continuously is a siren or an alarm, not music. Is your life a song or an alarm?

So here you are in your life. You've worked hard to get here. You spend mornings in a rush: to get your body clean, to eat your breakfast, maybe get kids off to school. You climb a mountain every morning, then rush off to work. People look to you for guidance. Maybe you're a leader. This day, you are sick of it all. If one more crabby person comes your way, you will scream. There's no satisfaction in your life anymore, just a vague deadness. Where is the enthusiasm you once had? Where is the happiness you thought would come from working hard? You berate yourself for not doing enough. You feel you are out of balance in your life. But you try to get all the work done by neglecting what's really important to you: your kids, your spouse, your soul. Now here you are, in that top position. Kind of empty, isn't it? But you don't know another way. So you continue on.

One method to find another way is through the simple act of monitoring your breathing. In any book on public speaking or relieving stress, deep breathing holds a prominent place. Far Eastern philosophy describes inhaling deeply as an avenue to Prana, a substance that is invisible but transforms one's inner experience. Prana also is described as the breath of life. When in balance, you experience it as energy in your body. To increase life force, breathe slowly and deeply to draw in the invisible force that brings increased relaxation and well-being.

The benefit of relaxation is that it widens the gaps between thoughts. When I say relaxation, I'm not talking about inaction. I'm talking about something that is counter-intuitive, like using one's ki in the strong arm exercise or driving a Jeep down a steep hill. If you drive down a steep, slippery road in a four-wheel-drive vehicle and start to slip, your automatic response may be to slam on the brakes. But if you do that, you will go faster down the hill and career out of control. To gain control, you must avoid using the brakes, shift to a lower gear, let the vehicle go where it will, and even accelerate to get a grip on the road. Just as in aikido, you go with the momentum of the vehicle rather than force it where it doesn't want to go. The tendency to want to gain control when in a difficult interaction causes us to stiffen up and get ready to fight or to flee. By avoiding this tensing and allowing yourself to be in the stillness by taking in slow, deliberate deep breaths, you allow a space for a message to be sent by your Intuitive Knower. Then what you want to say will be delivered as a warrior for peace.

The Intuitive Knower

When you're with a difficult person, the chattering of your mind, coupled with the fuel from your stress, drowns out the energy of your ki. Instead of the mind chatter and having to deal with your own stressors, you can wade through these to find the calm that gives you access to your Intuitive Knower.

Take a deep breath in through your nose and hold it to the count of three. Then exhale slowly through your mouth. The pause that follows your exhalation is where your Intuitive Knower lives. Your Intuitive Knower is the objective part of you that offers suggestions when you remember to still your thoughts long enough to direct your attention to it. If you revisit a time when you received a great idea, you will realize that it came from this source. I have proved it to myself hundreds of times. You can prove it to yourself by following Exercise 3 at the end of this chapter.

Your Intuitive Knower understands and protects your best interest and the best interest of others. It is a soft, quiet voice that reaches out to you when you are still. If you are sick or injured, your Intuitive Knower is there with an opportunity to receive infinite wisdom, patience, and love. Your Intuitive Knower will guide you about what to do in any situation that bothers you. It will provide you with an appropriate response to a difficult person that will promote the most beneficial outcome possible. You have your own answers within you. On different occasions, I've asked my Intuitive Knower, "What's bothering me today?" And I've received different answers:

- ❧ You are craving a day off.
- ❧ You want to finish that report.
- ❧ Pay attention to what you eat, and get some exercise.
- ❧ You have not found expression for hurt feelings.
- ❧ You need to make amends for yesterday.

At the beginning of each day, I listen for any messages. When you listen for messages from your Intuitive Knower, you immediately recognize the wisdom of the answer. There is a quickening in your body, a feeling of excitement. It's as if a light went on in a room. Sometimes, you'll find the message is to spend extra time with another individual. On other occasions it will be to give time to yourself. When this occurs, you may remember that you've been neglecting your body, mind, or soul. On one occasion, the message for me was a reminder to take calcium. Another time, the dogs needed a walk. Still another time, in the jungles of Ecuador, I received a message to change my life. Your messages will be great and small. They could remind you of the most mundane, obvious point, and they may point your life in an entirely new direction.

⤚ ⤚

What you think about expands, creates. There are no neutral thoughts. Quantum physics tells us that the physical world appears to be solid only because that is the group perception of it. In a sense, we all are thinking the world into existence because everything begins first as thought. We co-create with that invisible energy that connects us. What do you think is going to happen if you spend most of your time in thoughts of fear or judgment?

Now that we have discussed the important elements of energy and the Intuitive Knower, we are ready to move on to Chapter 2, in which we will examine the fear that leaves us confined in an ever-shrinking comfort zone. Until we recognize our entrapment and the fear that confines us, we cannot strive to move beyond it.

✌ ✌

Exercise 1: Connecting with a Difficult Person

Imagine a stream of clear light emanating from your lower abdomen and building a sphere of light around you, until you are surrounded by a ball of soothing, clear light. Expand your sphere gradually, until it is big enough to include both you and the person who is being difficult. Do this at home in your imagination, at work in a meeting, at the supermarket—anytime you want to try it. How does the experience feel? Have you noticed any results? Does the process become easier as you practice?

Exercise 2: Choosing Your Thoughts and Creating Emotions

Imagine a beautiful red rose growing on a bush in your garden. See yourself clipping it off the plant (leaving a long stem), filling a clear crystal bud vase with water, and placing the rose into the vase. Imagine observing the beauty of the flower and breathing in its lovely aroma. See the contrast of the colors: vivid red supported by a green stem.

Now, let that image go, and replace it with the image of a patch of gray cement at the side of a house. Standing on the cement and leaning against the yellow stucco of the house is a torn, brown grocery bag with dark grease stains. As you approach the bag, you smell its contents before you actually see what is inside. Your nose is filled with the smell of sour milk from the crushed milk carton and the stench of rotting beef left over from a dinner almost a week ago. When you stand before the wilting bag, you see the milk carton and putrid meat alongside dried coffee grounds, fermenting orange rinds, crushed egg shells, and a few unidentifiable items you decide not to inspect too closely.

Were you able to shift easily between the two images? I think most of us would say that we have an easy time either choosing our thoughts or switching them when we are guided. But when we worry about something and have a physical reaction of fear in the body, we feel stuck in it as if on a track. You have a built-in guide and coach. You may not be used to listening to this guide when under stress. At other times you might have experienced choosing what you will think about, such as if you are planning a meal and need to decide what groceries to buy, or making home repairs and thinking about what parts you will need for the job. Your thoughts are the most powerful things in creating your world as it is right now and as it will be.

Now think about your worst-case scenario with a difficult person. Run it through your imagination like a movie. What is the worst that could happen here? Imagine it. How does it make you feel? Next, imagine the best possible outcome. Imagine how it would be if this situation, temporarily stuck perhaps, turned out to be a blessing for all concerned. What would happen? Imagine yourself interacting ideally with this person. How does this experience feel?

Were you able to do these exercises in your imagination? When with a difficult person, you choose how you think, and this choice influences how you feel. When you find yourself thinking the worst, say to yourself: "I am responsible for my thoughts and feelings and I am seeing this differently."[5] Then switch your thoughts and images to create a best-case scenario.

Exercise 3: Contacting Your Intuitive Knower

Take a deep breath, be still, and ask your Intuitive Knower for the answer to the question "How can I increase my well-being and energy level?" (Or choose a question of your own.) Write your response on a piece of paper or in your notebook.

Each morning and evening, take a moment to contact your Intuitive Knower for messages. Give it five to ten minutes each time to respond.

Exercise 4: Increasing Your Life Force Energy

When you are feeling low on energy, try one or more of the following exercises to increase your life force:

* Take several deep breaths, preferably outside in the fresh air.
* If you are hungry, eat a fresh, nutritious meal of fruits or vegetables.
* Spend time with an animal or by a tree.
* Take a brisk walk by some trees or by rushing water.

You also increase your life force by focusing on love. To do so, complete the following sentence:

> "I feel love when. . . ." Using ten different endings, write out this sentence ten times. Notice how you feel after writing these sentences.

Exercise 5: Meeting an Important Teacher

There is someone in your life right now who has something important to teach you. He or she has been sent by your Intuitive Knower to show you something about yourself. To discover the message from your Intuitive Knower, write down the name of the most difficult person in your life. This person is your teacher. Your text book lies open before you. Your lesson has begun.

2

THE COMFORT ZONE

"Come to the edge of the cliff," he said. "We're afraid,"
they said. "Come to the edge of the cliff," he said.
"We're afraid," they said. "Come to the edge of the cliff,"
he said. They came. He pushed. They flew.

—Guillaume Apollinaire

Life shrinks or expands in proportion to one's courage.

—Anaïs Nin

Life is either a daring adventure or nothing.

—Helen Keller

Why not go out on a limb? That's where the fruit is.

—Will Rogers

Courage is resistance to fear,
mastery of fear—not absence of fear.

—Mark Twain, *Pudd'nhead Wilson*

*L*ion tamers have to be aware of the animal's continual fight
for dominance. If left unchecked, a dominant lion will repeatedly
compete for the top position by using aggression in the form of
clawing, pushing, loud growling, and biting. With tools, know-

ledge and experience, however, confident lion tamers know how to thwart a struggle for power. In the world of taming lions, the comfort zone reflects the lion tamer's understanding of the nature of wild animals, training, practice, and experience. The more skilled, confident, and resourceful the lion tamer, the larger the comfort zone.

With people, the struggle for power can be seen in competition—striving to get more money when no amount is ever enough, trying to be perfect, and vying for a position of ever-higher status. Such struggles inevitably put lives out of balance. In an encounter with a difficult person, the ideal is not to struggle for dominance but to maintain respect for yourself and the person who is being difficult. The first step in developing the skills necessary to handle a difficult person with competence is gaining the confidence and willingness to move beyond the less effective patterns you may have developed over the years, to venture beyond the familiar.

In this chapter, you will learn about the comfort zone, that place where you feel all is right with the world. For each of us, the zone is different. I feel most comfortable on my couch surrounded by pillows and plump blankets, eating Good and Plentys, petting my golden retriever, and reading a trashy novel. An hour later, I finish my book and turn on the TV. Three hours later, the comfort zone has become the dead zone: a lethargic, dull, lifeless place. Unlike the dead feeling that comes of trying to stay in your comfort zone, stretching it brings vitality, self-confidence, and satisfaction. After experiencing initial fear or frustration from beginning something new, you gradually become sure of your ability in almost any situation. By stretching your comfort zone—by dealing with difficult people rather than shrinking from them—you gain confidence and increase your peace of mind. In this chapter, we will look at examples of people struggling in the confines of their comfort zones. We will examine the techniques they use (or could use) to expand their comfort zones and attain greater self-confidence and success in their lives.

Fight or Flight in the Comfort Zone

In our everyday lives, each of us faces frustrating or scary "lions," those intimidating, sometimes angry people whom we recognize as a threat to our well-being. Our reaction to these people can resemble our reaction to a wild animal: We may cower, unsure whether to make a move or keep still, to yell or keep silent. We don't want to make the situation worse. This reaction is the fight or flight response, an automatic, physical and emotional response triggered by fear that lingers from our earliest days as a species when it literally helped our ancestors stay alive in a physically threatening environment. Many of us succumb to this instinctive response without questioning our reaction because we see the world as a place of unpleasant, unexpected, threatening events. Ironically, as we shrink back into the ever-smaller "safe" space, we find that our fear is greater than it would have been if we had ventured out.

I once encountered an intelligent, creative teenage boy who stopped going to school because of his fear of embarrassment. David was a sixteen-year-old sophomore whose main purpose in life became to stay in his comfort zone. At first, he avoided only the homework in one class. Then he felt he needed to avoid the class altogether to save himself from embarrassment because the teacher kept asking for his homework. His fear grew until he was down to half a day of school attendance, then no school at all. I asked him how he felt, staying at home and watching TV, wondering how to avoid facing daily fears and challenges. He replied:

> *Every day, I stay in bed as late as I can so I don't have to think about nothing. I sack out till one. My teacher, she used to hassle me about homework. I couldn't stand her. One day when I did turn in a paper, she said, real loud, "Well, what's the occasion?" The whole class laughed at me. I laughed, too, but I never went back. If I turn the TV off, I have to have the radio blastin' 'cause my mind trips, y'know? I dunno how I'm*

*gonna graduate. Mom hassles me when she gets home, and she
cries. She says I don't care about her. So I go to my room till
she crashes. Then I watch TV. I can't go back now. It's been too
long, y'know?*

David didn't know that he was choosing entrapment in his comfort zone. He knew only that he was not willing to return to school.
He saw no way to relieve his pain in that setting. In an effort to prevent his complete withdrawal from education, he was placed on
independent study. Then, when he couldn't bring himself to attend
even the weekly trips to the campus to pick up and drop off work,
he received home teaching. At first, David was too ashamed to talk
with a therapist about his difficulty. He needed more time in his
comfort zone to accept that things would not change for him without some action on his part. Eventually, he attended weekly counseling sessions. He was placed on medication for depression. Then
he enrolled at an adult education school. The classes were small
and his teachers nurturing, and David was pleased when he earned
his first A. Today, as an adult in his twenties, David continues to
earn credits toward his high school diploma while working part
time as a janitor in a bowling alley. His job is a small but important
step toward reentering society. With each step out of his comfort
zone, David becomes more confident and less fearful.

Expanding Your Comfort Zone

The cure for overcoming fear in people involves empowering
them, and one effective way to empower someone is to teach the
person other ways to respond in fight or flight situations. For a
child afraid to go to school, empowering may involve giving the
child quarters to call home. For someone afraid to give a speech,
empowering may involve joining a Toastmasters group. For someone learning to deal with difficult people, empowering involves
learning multiple ways to respond and developing a way of thinking about possibilities that breaks the cycle of having expectations
that dreadful things might happen.

The following discussion elaborates on several specific techniques you can use to expand your own comfort zone, a crucial step in learning how to handle difficult people. The techniques that I've found to be most effective are: recognizing that you feed either love or fear; keeping your focus off yourself; being willing to break your pattern; separating your reaction from yourself; having the courage to express difficult emotions and to say, "I'm sorry;" and practicing these techniques until they come to you naturally.

Recognize That You Feed Either Love or Fear

For your first task in expanding your comfort zone, I ask you to adopt the following belief as if it were true: There are only two emotions—love and fear—and you are perpetually feeding either one or the other.

Each of us is either in a state of some form of love (including joy, happiness, ease, well-being, abundance, authenticity) or some form of fear (including anger, worry, stress, frustration, anxiety). The response you give in a difficult situation feeds one or the other. Thus, for example, if you respond to angry verbal abuse with blaming, you cause the fear side to grow. Likewise, if you respond to anger with placating behavior, you also feed the fear. If your response is to extend love, you cause the fear side to decrease. Extending love can include setting boundaries and taking a stand without blaming or anger. A psychiatrist tells the story of a patient of his who was out of control in a padded room in a psychiatric ward. None of the staff members had been able to go near him, and the patient hadn't verbally responded to their requests that he stop thrashing and hitting. The physician went to the door of the room and said, "I'm scared that if I come in there you're going to hit me. I wonder if you're feeling as scared as I am." The patient replied, "I'm scared as hell, too." After that, the psychiatrist was able to have a conversation with him. By remembering that the patient was in a state of fear, the doctor could extend love in his thoughts and try to make a connection.

There rarely is a need to shrink from a difficult person. In fact, dealing with difficult people is easier than you may think. The real challenge is choosing the right attitude with which to approach the person. As St. Paul said, "Hate the sin. Love the sinner." Learn to separate the individual from the difficulty you associate with him. A person who is being difficult is in some form of a state of fear and, whether aware of it or not, is requesting help. He is seeking someone able to see beyond the hostility and to respond accordingly. It is your choice whether you drift into a state of fear. And if you do, you must understand that your own reaction is leading the communication deeper in fear.

Keep Your Focus off Yourself

I observed the following scene in a supermarket. A woman at the butcher counter wanted to buy fresh salmon. The man behind the counter said, "We don't have any salmon today." The woman replied indignantly, "What! I came all the way here for salmon! What do you mean, you don't have any?" The butcher replied, "Well, usually the salmon is delivered on Tuesdays, but this week there was no salmon. I have halibut steaks and fresh cod." The woman, even more agitated, countered, "Last time, you had salmon! I'm not leaving here until I get some salmon!" The butcher shrugged his shoulders. "I don't have any salmon today," he said, adding, "I won't have salmon until Thursday. I ordered salmon, but they didn't deliver any when they came on Tuesday. I can't give you what I don't have." Still, the woman persisted, "I came all the way here to get salmon, and I'm not leaving until I get salmon!" She spoke so loudly that a crowd began to gather. The conversation went on like this for several more minutes before the woman finally left in a huff. The butcher explained to everyone around him that he couldn't sell fish he didn't have. He repeated the explanation three times.

Unless you're on trial for a crime that you did not commit, resist the temptation to defend yourself. Remember that you're dealing with irrational fear. Know that the difficult person is not for the moment interested in hearing the details about your innocence in the situation. In this example, the butcher may have believed that repeating himself calmly could defuse the woman's anger. Perhaps he had had success with this method in the past. However, it clearly was making the woman madder, and the butcher seemed unable to attempt another, more effective tactic.

The butcher stayed within his comfort zone. He stayed with what was familiar. Instead, he could have dropped what wasn't working and said or done something different. For example, he could have remembered that the yelling was a manifestation of the woman's fear, checked his own response, put it aside, and then said, "I can see how important having salmon is to you. Let's discuss how we can solve this problem together." At that point, he could have chosen to go the extra mile with her. He could, for example, have called another local store to search for salmon. Whatever his decision, any choice other than repeating his claims of self-defense would have pushed the boundaries of his comfort zone.

Be Willing To Break Your Pattern

In this example, Marnie, the mother of a seven-year-old girl enrolled at one of my schools, was able to salvage her day by breaking a pattern. She stood in the rain waiting for the bus. The morning had been hectic, as usual. There had been another scene that morning over getting the child ready for school. Despite the difficulty, Marnie knew that she would be on time to work because, once again, she had skipped breakfast and left her own needs out of the morning chores. A single working mother, she had raised her daughter alone after a car accident had left the child disabled from a head injury. Standing at the bus stop, Marnie smoothed the crumpled front of her coat, and her eyes caught the run in her pantyhose. No, she thought, running for the Circle K, not today when I have a presentation to make. Two minutes later, holding the new package of stockings and waiting in line in the store, she glanced nervously out the window for her bus. It seemed to take forever to get to the counter. She imagined her boss seeing her arrive late and shuddered.

Finally, the clerk rang up her purchase. She fumbled for the correct change and found that she was short sixty cents. "Will you take a check?" she asked the clerk. "Sorry, lady. We don't accept checks." Noticing the bus out of the corner of her eye, she dropped the stockings and ran across the street. Climbing the steps of the bus, she realized that she wasn't sure if this was the bus that would take her to her office. "Is this the number 10?" she asked. The bus driver frowned. "No," he said, "it's the 12. That's why there's a huge sign in the front saying 10 to Center City." She started to explain, "I didn't see the sign becau—" "Look, lady," he interrupted, "just get on the bus or get off!" After taking a deep breath to keep herself from taking on the bus driver's anger, she paid her fare and took a seat. Three more passengers got on. One of them, a man in his seventies, asked the driver, "Do you go to Center City?" "Can't anyone read anymore?" the bus driver replied sarcastically without answering the question. "Yes, this is the bus that goes to Center City," the woman said to the elderly gentleman. She invited the man over to her by patting the seat next to her. "Our bus driver seems to be having a bad day," she added.

Feeling a little better, she got off the bus two blocks from her office and called to say that she would be getting organized for the day over a plate of French toast. The woman got herself unstuck by doing little things to break out of her comfort zone. First, she acknowledged to herself that the bus driver's anger had nothing to do with her. Then, she helped the elderly man. The good feelings from this act improved her mood, enabling her to break out of her routine of arriving at her office every day at the same time. When she got to work, she felt ready to perform and was more efficient because she had been careful to set her priorities. Her boss was predictably grouchy, but the experience of expanding her comfort zone had left her feeling confident and able to deal with him.

Separate Your Reaction from Yourself

Separating the physical reaction you get from how you respond can be as simple as acknowledging its presence and letting it be as it is. An example of separating yourself from your reaction is to silently acknowledge to yourself, "I'm in my own 'stuff' now, so I know I'll just make this worse if I blame how I feel on the situation or an individual," or to say out loud, "I may look angry as I say this. That's because I'm scared." Or "I'm really mad, and I know it's my own 'stuff,' not you doing it to me." Another way to do this is to think silently to the physical feeling, as if it were a person giving you a warning. You might "say" to it, "Thank you for the warning, but I want to help this woman." Or you might promise to give it some attention later. When you acknowledge your "stuff" as your own unfinished business, you have effectively removed it from the equation.

Have the Courage to Express Difficult Emotions and to Say, "I'm Sorry"

Stretching your comfort zone applies also to communicating difficult emotions and apologizing to someone you know you have hurt. For many people, the most difficult feelings to express are negative emotions (which are forms of fear). Others find it more difficult to communicate feelings of love. It takes courage for these people each time they express their true selves. Many of us also find it difficult to say, "I'm sorry," even when we feel regret. Apologizing calls for the same kind of courage required to stand up to an abuser. With practice, however, expressing your emotions becomes easier, and the rewards are great. Those times when you are aware of either a feeling of regret or one of love and caring, instead of holding back, find a way to express it. Override your hesitation.

Practice, Practice, Practice

Perhaps the most important element of expanding your comfort zone is developing your skills through practice. The beginning stages we all go through when developing any new skill are inevitably awkward and not much fun. Consider the following experience of a novice skier.

Phase 1. His bindings are too loose, and he loses one of his skis. He huffs and puffs, overheated in his turtleneck, bulky sweater, and ski jacket. Determined to arrive at the appointed place for his first ski lesson, he hobbles on one foot, carrying the wayward ski. Snow is bunched up at his waistband, a souvenir from his latest fall. The heat from his body makes it drip maddeningly down his pants. Balancing the ski on one shoulder, he leans to the left and shakes the bulk of the snow out of his pants. The ski slips off and plunges so deeply into the snow that it remains sticking up. He pulls the ski from the snow, repositions it on his shoulder, and struggles on to his appointment. His face red from the effort, he at last arrives at the ski school. Ten minutes later, he is snowplowing down a slope for beginners, the instructor calling at his heels, "Keep zee knees bent und zee veight on zee downhill ski."

Phase 2. He has had six lessons, he can take his skis on and off without assistance, and he can correctly adjust his bindings. He can carry both skis on one shoulder without dropping them. He gets to the slope, sits on the chairlift without falling, exits the chairlift in a heap, and is buried by subsequent riders. He snowplows down the hill, loses control when he picks up too much speed, and runs over another skier, who shouts, "Watch where you're going!" Afterward, he walks to the lodge for hot chocolate and a glazed doughnut.

Phase 3. One year later, he's doing stem turns and traversing intermediate slopes skillfully. Sometimes, though, he picks

up more speed than he can handle and runs into trees or peo-
ple unfortunate enough to be in his path.
    Phase 4. After two years, he skis parallel down any slope.
No longer is he bumbling around on bunny slopes. Now he can
enjoy the fruits of his earlier labors. Most important of all, he
never has to go through the first three phases again.

When you're trying one of the techniques recommended in this
book for dealing with difficult people, be patient with yourself. If
you have some awkward moments in between your successes, just
keep going. Don't give up. Before long, you'll be effective automatically, creating peace out of chaos.

In my six-week workshops, participants select one person or
situation to address during the course, trying out new skills before
taking them out into the world. We practice each step first in the
safety of the class. In the following example, we see how one
woman was able—through practice in a workshop environment—
to build up the confidence necessary for her to confront her
estranged husband in a positive, productive manner.

Carla, forty-four-year-old general manager in a Fortune 500
Company, wanted to end her fourteen-year marriage. Her husband
Jerry, was both verbally and physically abusive. Although they had
been separated for more than a year, she feared setting off his rage
and avoided discussing divorce arrangements with him. In the past,
he had become extremely angry if she even mentioned legalities.
She had learned well to contain her real self and tiptoe around his
feelings with polite words.

Carla had rehearsed leaving her comfort zone in a role play in
which she met with Jerry at her favorite restaurant. Carla's voice is
naturally much softer than Jerry's, so she practiced with others in
the class to raise the volume of her voice. Then, picking a man in
the class to represent her spouse, she went over what she would say
to Jerry, refining it as she went along. At first, her fear was so great
that she had difficulty even pretending, but she kept practicing,
remembering how she feels when managing her team of ten engineers. In the work setting, she has no trouble giving directions and

taking charge. With Jerry, however, she had learned to keep a low profile to avoid his anger and criticism. I knew that with enough repetition and planning, Carla could have the ideal discussion in the workshop with her "husband." Over the next two weeks, he gave her his worst, and Carla learned how to handle herself in a way that felt comfortable to her.

Finally, the day came when Carla met her husband. After their steaming omelets arrived, she began the conversation. "Jerry, I want to complete our separation into a divorce. I am ready to go on in my life, and I need to have our divorce finalized. I appreciate how good you are with Donald (their son), and I will remember the good times we had together. I forgive you, and I forgive myself for the troubles we had." To her surprise and delight, Jerry did not rage. He tried to talk her out of divorce, but she kept her ground. Her ability to remain calm surprised her.

If you don't have the benefit of a workshop environment to practice in, you can do this kind of practice in your mind, or you can write it out as dialogue on paper. You can imagine your worst-case scenario, and come up with several responses to your difficult person that leave you feeling good about the encounter. By imagining the worst and then creating your response to it, you empower yourself to face almost any situation.

An Example of Venturing Out

When you begin to test the boundaries of your comfort zone, you can select difficult people to experiment with. Recently, I came across a difficult person on the levee above the bicycle trail and made the conscious decision to try my developing skills in dealing with him. He was with a crew of workers, engaged in labor with heavy equipment. I needed to get to the street beyond the levee because I was headed for my favorite coffee shop to edit one of these chapters over a cappuccino. After dragging my bicycle from the trail up to the levee, I saw there was a steep downhill dirt path to my right. I also saw that there was enough room to go straight ahead, around the workers' equipment. I chose the latter route, but

I soon knew that it was a poor choice, as one of the workers quickly pointed out, abandoning his tractor to set me straight. With one hand on his hip and the other waving a screwdriver, he communicated more to me than his request that I take the other path. "You!" he shouted at me. "Get out of here! The bicycle trail is down there!" He was so angry that he was spitting when he shouted. His colleagues laughed scornfully.

Now, I am a firm believer in expressing anger, but not if the anger is expressed as blaming rather than being owned. (I will address this point further in Chapter 5, "Healing the Inner Lion.") I felt surprised, then angry. My pattern when I become angry is either to swallow my anger and say nothing or to explode in anger myself. Normally, in a situation like this one, either I would have gone on and not responded to my anger or his, or I would have blasted him in kind. Both of those responses are "easy." But this time, in my mind, I separated my anger from the situation at hand. Recognizing his fear state (maybe he thought I would get hurt) and realizing that he was right about my choosing the wrong path, but not wanting to accept his rage without standing up for myself, I responded, speaking out in a volume that matched his: "Yes, excuse me."

He told me that I had no right to be there and asked if I was too stupid to recognize the bike trail. "The bike trail's down there," he added sarcastically, pointing importantly to the meandering path ten feet below. His three co-workers laughed again.

I turned my bike to head down the steeper slope, feeling put down, but I did not want to leave the scene without responding, so I delivered a statement of my own. I might have chosen to let the opportunity go by, but I wanted to express myself fully in what I assessed was a safe situation, and I wanted to take the opportunity to practice. My choice had to do with not wanting any residual anger to linger and interfere with my writing. Much of our frustration with difficult people comes from being misunderstood or not delivering our truth. I didn't need or expect him to change in any way. I recognized his temporary state of fear and felt compassion for whatever in his life caused him to rage so easily. He was beginning to climb back into his tractor when I issued my reply: "I am glad to go around. I'm sorry I startled you. Your sarcasm wasn't necessary."

I said it loud enough so that I could feel the comforting presence of my own power. If further invalidation came from him, it wouldn't matter. I had made the choice to not shrink back and knew that I did so without adding fuel. I knew that I had the right to make a mistake. I knew that I had the right to be treated with respect.

He leaned out of the tractor, startled. "What?" he shouted, climbing back out. I met his volume. "I said that I am happy to go around. You didn't need to be nasty to get me to do that." With an astonished look on his face, he said, "I'm sorry."

🔊 🔊

Some of us find it natural to withdraw from conflict and other situations that leave us feeling uncomfortable. Others tend to lash out in anger. But each time we choose either of those options, we make the same behavior in ourselves and in those we perceive as difficult more likely in the future. The price we pay for this behavior is a growing— although perhaps subconscious—fear in us. More and more, we find ourselves less able to speak up for ourselves in a way that moves toward conciliation. Shrinking back and lashing out in anger are both fear responses. We lack the confidence to follow the path that leads to our personal happiness and success. Our lives become increasingly narrow and unsatisfying. By consciously observing where the boundaries to our comfort zone lie and deliberately working to push those boundaries out through positive action, we can build the confidence necessary to improve our relationships with difficult people and improve the quality of our lives as we do so.

The next step in developing your lion taming skills is recognizing the hazard of characterizing people as difficult in the first place. Chapter 3 shows you not only the harm of characterizing others but what your characterizations of other people actually reveal about yourself.

⚞ ⚟

Exercise: Finding and Expanding Your Comfort Zone Boundaries

We all live in a comfort zone. Some are large and reflect our confidence and positive outlook; others are small and confining because we let fear play too large a role in our lives. To find the limits of your comfort zone, circle any of the items below that make you feel uneasy. Then try out those you have circled to determine the boundaries of your own comfort zone and to become familiar with how you feel as you push the boundaries outward. The easier it is for you to perform these exercises, the greater your comfort zone. If you do not like the sensation you get when beginning to expand your comfort zone, remind yourself that this feeling is OK.

1. Ask a stranger for directions.
2. Figure something out for yourself instead of asking for help.
3. Praise someone for the service he or she gives you in a restaurant, grocery store, or other location.
4. Ask your waiter or waitress to have your soup reheated.
5. Attend a meeting of a club that has interested you but that you have been reluctant to join.
6. Accept an invitation to speak before a group.
7. Allow a silence of at least ten seconds in a conversation with a friend.
8. Identify a pattern in your daily life (such as talking too much, talking too little, letting bills pile up, paying bills as soon as they arrive), and consciously break it every day for a week. Keep a record of how the experience feels.
9. Ask a loved one to acknowledge you for something of which you are proud.
10. Tell someone about a time you looked foolish.

11. Tell someone about a time you looked great.
12. At a gathering in which your opinion differs from the opinion of everyone else, speak your opinion.
13. Speak your differing opinion without blaming others for theirs.
14. Wear a silly hat.
15. Wear mismatched socks.
16. Tell someone important to you how much you care about him or her.
17. Give honest feedback if someone asks you for it.
18. Respond to a criticism by agreeing with it.
19. Apologize to someone.
20. Ask someone to forgive you.
21. Tell someone how grateful you are.
22. Express your hurt feelings to the person involved.
23. Tell someone how frustrated you are.
24. Go through a whole day without complaining.
25. Volunteer to do something extra.
26. Eliminate one activity from your life.
27. If the dress code at your office is informal, wear a suit and tie to work.
28. If the dress code at your office is formal, wear jeans to work.
29. Stay an hour longer than your usual quitting time at work.
30. Leave an hour earlier than your usual time.

Is there a pattern to the ones you circled? Do they involve asking someone for something? Is it the possibility of looking foolish that stops you? Do you believe you shouldn't make mistakes? Is it expressing love? Or expressing frustration? In my classes, many of the men say they have the most difficulty expressing love. These men have an easier time expressing negative emotions than positive ones. Many of the women say they have an easier time expressing love than negative emotions. A few men and women have trouble with both.

After a few trials of comfort zone expansion, write down in your journal the sensation you get as you venture out. Write down where it is located in your body and what your thoughts are about it. To put an end to the uncomfortable sensation in yourself, reframe the feeling in your mind. Give it a positive label, such as "Yes!," "Growth," "Muscle," "Courage," "Brave," or "Warrior." Write this word in big letters in your journal.

Be willing to be in the presence of fear. Allow fear a place in your comfort zone.

3

REMOVING THE MASK OF THE LION

*Everything that irritates us about others
can lead us to an understanding of ourselves.*
—Carl G. Jung

*Gained without effort, discovered like a treasure
in my house, my enemy is to be appreciated
as a helper on the path to Enlightenment.*
—Santideva, *Entering the Path of Enlightenment*

*I*magine that you came across a lion out of his cage while you are visiting the circus. What is your judgment going to be about this lion? If you're the lion trainer for the circus, you will have a notably different reaction than you would if you're someone who is afraid of house cats. If you are unfamiliar with the ways of lions and inexperienced with handling them, you would likely focus on the animal's fangs and claws and assume the worst about the lion's intentions and your own likelihood to escape the encounter unharmed. A trainer familiar with the lion might be able to lead the lion back to its cage without incident. Someone who simply panicked at the sight of the animal might turn and run— the worst possible choice because it likely would trigger the animal's instinctual response to pursue fleeing prey. With people, our reactions can be similarly reactive and similarly based on fear (although, lucky for us, rarely to such an extent). When we assume the worst based on our limited understanding of a person, we needlessly view the words and actions of that person through a false filter of misperception.

In learning about our judgments and how they limit what happens between us and the lions in our lives, we obtain the ability to remove them. Then we are able to recognize that the person we consider to be difficult is more than his behavior. This chapter examines how our negative characterizations of difficult people influences our relationship with them and provides specific techniques to help you to avoid characterizing others.

Characterization Creates Difficult People

In our relationship with difficult people, our fear and misunderstanding take the form of judging called characterization. A characterization is a negative judgment about someone that influences what you say and think about that person. Negative judgments create a mask that obscures the true image of the person. They prevent you from recognizing the sum total of that person's being. That is, because you've already judged the person, your perception filters out everything that doesn't fit in with who you've already decided that person is. Then, whenever that person is in your presence, you will tend to notice only those qualities that seem to fit your judgment.

One hot summer day, I was summoned from the backyard to take a telephone call from Sylvia. Although she intended the call to be friendly and supportive, I found it annoying. She is too friendly—so much so that her friendliness seems inauthentic. I hear in her words and in her tone an unspoken pleading: "Please like me and think I'm special." This time, she was calling to offer me assistance. Earlier, I had told her about a large project I was working on. Now she wanted to hear about my struggle and prove her friendship to me by helping me complete the job. I had already completed it, though—and enjoyed myself while I was working on it. She seemed anxious to hear about my difficulty and seemed a little disappointed (and perhaps a little disbelieving) when I told her how well it all had gone. I knew as I spoke with her that even if I hadn't completed the job yet, I wouldn't have wanted her help.

In the past, when I shared my characterization of Sylvia with someone, I would say such things as "I get so irritated with her! Always the smile on the face, the silent pleas to like her." And the other person would say, "Oh, me, too! When she said. . . ." And then the person I was talking with would add her own characterization of Sylvia to mine. You know how it goes. We all have been in similar situations. The mask we had made for her, our combined characterization, was then a little more opaque, a little more firmly in place. Hidden somewhere behind those two characterizations was the real Sylvia.

If I share my characterization of her with you and then introduce you to her, what do you think you would notice? Would it be her competence? Her guilelessness? Her vast capacity to love? Her knack with words? Chances are, when you met Sylvia you would see only my characterization of her. You would look for her to plead to be liked or to be thought of as special. Chances are that nearly everything she would say or do would somehow fall under these labels. I will have contaminated your perception with my characterization.

For most of my life, this sort of discussion came so naturally to me that I never gave it a thought. It never occurred to me that there would be a time when I would object to it and not want to participate in it. I understand that we cannot avoid talking about the people who are a part of our lives. Why would we want to? We are all interested in each other, in the choices we and our loved ones make, and in the significant events in our lives. But there is a better way. At first, after I stopped participating in such discussions, I missed the intimacy generated by talking about other people and their secrets and difficulties, but I replaced it by sharing tales of my own secrets and difficulties. I also noticed during conversations in which others were being judgmental that when I didn't join them in their characterization, they were grateful for the chance to see things differently. I realized then that no one likes to judge another. Deep down we all realize that it is we who suffer from the judgment, so anything that helps us get unstuck from our characterization is welcomed. Although I feared initially that I would lose closeness with my friends, I found instead that the trust between us deepened.

In the following example, I negatively characterized a difficult person and predictably made a bad situation worse.

One day, I was driving on the cobblestone streets of Old Sacramento with my youngest daughter, who was then sixteen. We were looking for a parking space. Trying to fit my own vehicle into a parking space that was too small, I blocked a side street that another driver wanted to turn down. He was obviously in a hurry and furious that I was blocking him. He shouted angrily at me, alternating between shaking his fist at me and banging it on his steering wheel. I couldn't move because his car was crossing the only path I could take. I absently thought, "It's OK. I can handle this, I know how to deal with people who are angry. I'm in a good mood." Still, I got that prickly, queasy feeling in my body—the feeling that usually leads me to either flee the scene or stay and fight. (I have learned not to trust this feeling, which is an important early step in learning to deal effectively with difficult people. Often, we believe that we're under attack when we're in the presence of this feeling.)

As if it had a mind of its own, the middle finger of my left hand, the one closest to the window and the one most visible to the other driver, rose and shook itself mockingly at this already enraged and red-faced man. For a moment, I felt exhilarated. Maneuvering my car back into the street, I headed off to find a larger parking space. Through tight lips, my wise daughter said, "I can't believe you did that! You could have gotten us hurt or killed!"

When I pulled into a parking space three blocks away, the man drove by slowly, having gone out of his way to find me, and shook his middle finger at me. Then he circled around so he could pass my way again and gestured again, this time even more emphatically. (Someone witnessing only the latter half of our interaction would think that I was the victim.)

If I had seen him again later that day, after my temper had cooled, I would have said, "I'm sorry that I was so rude to you. I'm sure that's the last thing you needed!" As it was, I merely nodded my head and smiled sheepishly.

Sam Keen's poem *To Create an Enemy* illustrates how we help to create difficult people with judgment, imposing the parts of ourselves we deny onto the difficult person.

To Create an Enemy
by Sam Keen[1]

Start with an empty canvas
Sketch in broad outline the forms of
men, women, and children.
Dip into the unconscious well of your own
disowned darkness
with a wide brush and
stain the strangers with the sinister hue
of the shadow.
Trace onto the face of the enemy the greed,
hatred, carelessness you dare not claim as
your own.
Obscure the sweet individuality of each face.
Erase all hints of the myriad loves, hopes,
fears that play through the kaleidoscope of
every finite heart.
Twist the smile until it forms the downward
arc of cruelty.
Strip the flesh from bone until only the
abstract skeleton of death remains.
Exaggerate each feature until man is
metamorphosed into beast, vermin, insect.
Fill in the background with malignant
figures from ancient nightmares—devils,
demons, myrmidons of evil.
When your icon of the enemy is complete

you will be able to kill without guilt,
slaughter without shame.
The thing you destroy will have become
merely an enemy of God, an impediment
to the sacred dialectic of history.

Although Keen is writing of the extreme characterizations that allow groups to rise up and kill one another, the process he describes is similar to the process each of us regularly goes through, although generally we are unaware of it, when we interact with difficult people. As Keen describes, we may project on the other person an aspect of ourselves that we have denied. Denial such as this can lead to harmful consequences, from mistrust to violence.

On reflection, I can see denial in my relationship with Sylvia. If I ask myself why she irritates me so much and I am willing to look inside, I will find something bubbling up to be healed, something totally mine. As I scan my past, I realize that I have looked and sounded just like this—wanting to be accepted, increasing my friendliness even when my advances were obviously unwelcome. I denied this feeling because I preferred to think of myself as someone who has inner strength and who does not need the approval of others to feel good about the way I choose to live my life. The reality, of course, is that both the strength and the need for approval are parts of me.

If we remove our characterization and acknowledge that what we think we see in another is actually a reflection of ourselves, then we move from reaction (fear) to an action (love) of empathizing. We imagine how the other person feels, responding with compassion instead of judgment. These are both forms of projecting ourselves onto another, but the latter is done in a conscious way, by imagining ourselves in the other's shoes.

Regarding my finger-shaking trip to Old Sacramento, I could say that I have no explanation for my behavior, but I know better. My response came from my own well of "stuff" that I had buried. (When we are in the presence of our own "stuff," we may feel that someone is victimizing us, not realizing that it's our own reaction to the situation that is causing the stress. To learn more about "stuff"—how to identify it and how to heal it—see Chapters 4, 5, and 6.) Several things happened during the encounter: First, I felt an automatic response of shame because someone was angry with me. Then I felt anger because I believed that I was being treated abusively. These combined to trigger my fight or flight response. In this case, my choice was to fight. Last, I characterized the other driver. I decided that he was a jerk.

What You Say Matters

Not only does your judgment make a difference, but what you say to others to characterize a difficult person based on your perception matters. As I indicated in my tale of Sylvia above, such conversations have an impact. In the following example, in which well-intended people made negative judgments about a child's parents, the potential for harm was considerably greater.

Katie was ten-years-old and having trouble in school. She couldn't seem to get her homework turned in, and she arrived at school disheveled each day. Usually, her clothes had holes, and her long, dark hair was uncombed. When other students made attempts at friendliness, Katie would run to the corner, sit down, curl up, and rock back and forth. The school requested an evaluation. She was new to our district but had been attending the school for three months, long enough to adjust to the new environment. She just "couldn't keep up with the class," her teacher explained, frustrated. Katie would cry at recess without provocation.

"I think something's going on in that home," one teacher said, shaking her head, shortly before our first meeting with Katie's parents. Catching the drift of the conversation, another joined in: "Yes, yesterday she stayed in the classroom crying and wouldn't come out even though I sent her friend Melissa to help." The first teacher added, "She reminds me of Krissy. Her father used to beat her when he was drinking. I had to report him to Child Protective Services." After a pause, she added, "Her dress was torn when she came in yesterday." Two more people came to join the meeting. The conversation continued although the late joiners didn't know that the topic of discussion was not the family that was the focus of the meeting.

It was ten minutes after twelve, the hour when the meeting was scheduled to begin. I was beginning to buy into the stories being shared. I expected the parents to arrive with false smiles that hid their dark tendencies. "We can't very well teach them if the parents don't even care enough to come to a meeting," one person sighed. Others nodded in agreement. Our characterization of Katie's parents suggested that they were child beaters. Of course, they were late. They probably didn't care enough even to show up.

At fifteen minutes past the hour, a man walked into the room. He was holding a piece of paper sent to him by Katie's teacher, on which he had written his concerns about his daughter. I noticed, at the top of the page, the time the teacher had written down for the meeting: 12:15.

The meeting began. The unknowing parent saw only our polite smiles and didn't know that we were now inspecting him through the filter of our characterization. Good manners covered unspoken judging and blaming. One teacher, reading from her own report on the girl, said, "Katie has been seated in the front of the classroom and paired with another, higher functioning student for reading." She added that Katie was performing at grade level in math, and that she was three years behind grade expectations in spelling. The discussion focused on the dry evaluations in our folders. I kept thinking about the earlier conversation—such a contrast to this one! I didn't want to leave it unmentioned, but I didn't want to share it, either. I felt ashamed to have listened to it all and worse, to have said nothing in his defense. I felt like an accomplice to a crime, unjustly indicting this man with made-up evidence. Finally, one of our group broached the subject: "Katie has been crying at recess time," her teacher began. "Does she say anything about this at home?"

"Yes, I know," he said solemnly. "When I lost my job in the Bay Area, she and her brother didn't want to move here. Katie had a lot of friends there, but her best friend died of leukemia. Her brother has adjusted to the move, but Katie feels alone here and grieves for Jenny. My wife and I try to make it better by being together in the evenings and helping her talk about her feelings."

Later, I asked Katie's teacher about his earlier assumption regarding the girl's home life. Embarrassed now that he had met the parent, he regretted that he had made judgments based on little information. Still, he reminded me, his intention had been to help Katie. Two people in our group had heard only the characterization. They never met Katie's father, so they went away with their misperceptions intact. The rest of us felt ashamed after that meeting.

Gossiping Builds Characterizations

A specific type of talk that we all participate in that can cause great harm to our personal relationships is gossiping. Gossiping serves two roles: to make the gossiper feel OK by putting someone else down and to make an intimate connection with another person. Ironically, it is a longing for closeness and validation that makes us want to attack those who are not present. In the following example, I am reminded of the power of gossip.

"I don't know what to do," I began after we ordered our salads. Three friends listened to my story about the difficulty I was having with a colleague. Early on in my acquaintance with her, I had detected a coolness in her presence and took it as evidence that I had done something wrong. Feeling uneasy about it, I seemed to notice other evidence of her dislike toward me: a frown on her face that seemed directed at me and silence or short comments to me when she had animated converations with others. I felt shame and guilt. I increased my friendliness, but she withdrew even further from me. Even when she told me that she would prefer to be left alone, I continued to write notes and attempt conversations. Her behavior toward me was a lot like my behavior toward Sylvia. Because of my fear, I perceived the problem to be huge. I grew afraid to go to work. I became obsessed with trying to fix it.

At lunch, I presented myself as the victim of a person who was hard to get along with. I sought comfort and support from my friends. I am forever grateful to the friend who gently said to me in the middle of my story, "Remember the gestalt." The gestalt is the whole of things. To remember the gestalt is to imagine that the person you are talking about is there with you and to imagine how she would feel about what you are saying. Gestalt therapy focuses on understanding all the parts of the story so that you can see the bigger picture. When I imagined what I would have been saying with the person present, the tone and content of what I said changed. I focused more on my reaction than on blaming.

Ten years after this restaurant scene, I met with the same friends, and one of them told me that she was serving on a committee with the person I had spoken to them about and that she has never been able to feel completely free of the picture I painted of the person. Even though I had gone back and corrected what I had said—that is, taken responsibility for the difficulty I was having—my characterization years before still contaminated her perception of the woman.

I overheard the following discussion in a restaurant. In this example, we can see how two people during the course of a regular conversation can, through their gossiping, build each other's characterization of someone, in this case, their boss:

> *First man: I think he's losing it. Yesterday, he called to find out why Carl hadn't attended his staff meeting. I told him that Carl had another meeting scheduled that he couldn't get out of. He said if it happens again, he'll have me fire him. Can you believe it? I can't do that.*
>
> *Second man: Whoa! He said that? He told me that I wasn't measuring up this year. Can you believe that? I'm working twelve-hour days, and he tells me it's not good enough. Said I need to be more aggressive. He won't be satisfied until I'm as miserable as he is. I have a family!*

Although gossiping provided some intimacy for the two friends, it cost them well-being in their relationship with their boss. There are other ways to develop intimacy and discuss fears. For example, by expressing your own truth, you can increase the level of intimacy for everyone in a conversation. You could express aspects of yourself that used to be sources of difficulty but that you have now accepted: "I know how controlling I can get when I feel stressed," or "Today, I seem to be easily irritated." (Expressing feelings of love also increases intimacy: "I'm so glad to have you in my life" and "I want to spend some time with you.") Consider the following option, which the first man could have chosen:

> *First man: I'm faced with the possibility of having to fire an employee I care about. This is one of the parts of my job where when I'm told what to do, I don't agree with it, but I feel I have to follow orders.*
> *Second man: Who is it?*
> *First man: I don't want to say who. I'm bringing it up because I've been stressed all week about this. What bothers me most about it is having to face him.*

Instead of gossiping about an employee or blaming his boss, he focuses on his own experience. Or consider the following exchange and a different response from the second man:

> *First man: I think he's losing it. Yesterday, he called to find out why Carl hadn't attended his staff meeting. I told him that Carl had another meeting scheduled that he couldn't get out of. He said if it happens again, he'll have me fire him. Can you believe it? I can't do that.*
> *Second man: That's a tough spot to be in. What have you considered doing so far?*

It's possible to listen without adding to the characterization, to help someone through a difficult spot and bring about release. (The second man also could have asked, "How is that affecting you?") You may gain momentary intimacy by feeding each other's characterizations, but you lose in the long run. You lose well-being in your body. You lose your integrity. When you feed others' judgments, you feed the fear.

Alternatives to Characterization

In the following example, characterizing could have occurred but didn't, because I had my mind enthusiastically focused elsewhere. I was driving down a main street alone on my birthday and impulsively decided to take myself to lunch. After I turned left by the five-by-three-foot "No Left Turn" sign, a police officer on a motorcycle invited me to pull over. My internal response was one of joy—quite inappropriate to the occasion, you might be thinking. It is common in situations like this to feel fear, anger, guilt, or possibly regret. However, at a conference on the use of humor, I had gotten an idea that I wanted to try out if I was ever pulled over.

A permanent frown seemed etched into the officer's face as he approached my car. I eagerly rolled down my window and greeted him with a smile. I couldn't have been more pleased to have been pulled over and given an opportunity to use humor with a difficult person. My smile and pleasure at being in this officer's presence were absolutely genuine. I was extending love to him in my thoughts. With a ticket pad in his left hand and his pencil poised to write, he opened his mouth to speak. Before he said a word, though, I spoke up with a line I had waited three years to say. "I'll have a hamburger, french fries, and a vanilla shake," I ordered, not caring how much the ticket would cost. Any amount would be worth the research I was conducting for this book. In the back of my mind, I remembered that the speaker who introduced me to the idea of using this approach had added the disclaimer, "I don't recommend doing this." I watched the officer with interest.

Traffic was light, so he didn't have to be concerned about how he might be appearing in front of others. I was willing to take the responsibility of paying any fines for breaking the law. Here we were, two human beings having an interaction. I was feeling calm, indulging myself on my birthday, thinking, Isn't this wonderful?

He started to speak, and I interrupted with "No, make that a cheeseburger with fries and a shake." His downturned mouth turned into a straight line before he asked me for my driver's license. You couldn't really call it smile, and it was there for only the slightest moment before his mouth returned to its original position. In that split second, though, I knew we had connected.

He pointed to the "No Left Turn" sign. His frown deepened. I waited, pleased with my accomplishment, feeling complete. "The sign is big, isn't it?" I asked. The officer wrote something with his pencil, then paused. Finally, he said, "Be more careful next time," and put his pad away. I suppose I was glad not to get a ticket. If I had gotten one, though, I would have a souvenir from a moment in my life that I would not want to trade. There was no characterization and no appearance of my "stuff" in that experience.

The point of this story is that your internal state adds to either the fear pool or the love pool. How you perceive anything is a choice. By removing your characterization, you affect how you interact with difficult people and difficult situations.

Removing Characterizations

It may take time—a day, a week, a year—but the thoughts you send out today will create results in your future. Countless books are available on what to do with negative thought patterns, from the religious viewpoint of Norman Vincent Peale's *The Power of Positive Thinking* to psychiatrist David Burns' book *Feeling Good: The New Mood Therapy* to physician Deepak Chopra's concept of "bodymind" in *Ageless Body, Timeless Mind*. Thoughts are the most powerful things in the world. Look around you. Everything you see was once a thought in someone's head. Even nature, I believe, is a thought in the mind of the energy that created it, just as we are thoughts in that same "mind."

We co-create with that same energy, starting first with our thoughts, which then manifest into action and results. To think is to create. The way this works in our relationships with difficult people is that when you send out a negative thought, you are the one to experience its effect. (In the same way, when you give love, it is you who feels its presence.) Because you are constantly thinking, you are perpetually creating your life around you. This book is an example of this process. It began as an idea in my mind when I became excited by the dramatic results I saw as I tried out different techniques and began the process of healing my "stuff." My thoughts shifted from fear (stewing and fretting over that relationship) to love (creating).

To help myself remove characterizations, I have memorized the following sentences:

- Do I recognize that this person is bigger than whatever he is stuck in for the moment?[2]
- Do I recognize that I'm bigger than any of my own "stuff" that I'm stuck in right now?
- What would I say if I were going to die tomorrow?
- What would I say if this person were on his deathbed right now?
- Imagine this person being loved by someone, such as his mother.
- Find something admirable about this person. For example, is he passionate, single-minded, or talented?
- Think about a context in which this person's behavior would be an asset.

We leap to conclusions all the time and don't think it matters. We make judgments based on so little information! Too easily, we make unkind judgments about situations that we don't understand. Just as forgiveness releases the one doing the forgiving and love is felt by the one loving, if you are not getting the respect you desire, chances are you are not being respectful. Check to see if you are talking behind another's back or if you are negatively judging the person. When you begin to change what you do and say behind the scenes with the difficult people in your life, you will begin to witness first hand the improvement in the difficult relationships.

~~ ~~

Dealing with difficult people is dealing with their fear. Most people who create pain are unaware that they are doing so. As you deal with their rejection or criticism, you are really dealing with your own doubt and fear. The difficult person is a catalyst that brings your own wounds to the surface. Often, when you change your way of responding, the difficult person changes his response to you. Removing characterizations is the place to start making that change. When you've removed your judgments and characterizations from your heart, when you have removed the mask you've made for those people you call difficult, you will find yourself interacting with people more openly and honestly. Your mere presence will be an extension of love and will be felt by the difficult person. Such a change doesn't happen overnight, though. It happens gradually as you heal your bag of "stuff." In the following exercise, you are asked to examine the characteristics of a few of the people in your life whom you consider to be difficult. That exercise will prepare you for the next three chapters, which focus on identifying and healing the "stuff" in your life.

~~ ~~

Exercise: Taking Stock

Difficult people are the mediators between conscious and unconscious parts of the personality. Whom do you dislike or judge negatively? This exercise gives you the opportunity to look at the characterizations that affect your view of others.

On the left side of a piece of paper or in your notebook, make a list of a few difficult people in your life. They may be family members, friends, those you work with, clients, or customers. On the right side of the page, list the characteristics that bother you.

Here's an example of how your page may look:

Person	Characteristics
Jerry	Plays the victim role ("Poor me")
	Judges me/Is critical
Carmine	Is depressed
	Sucks up too much of my time
	Acts like she's fragile and has others walking on eggs
Lonny	Is too dependent
	Compares himself with others
	Is more comfortable when I'm failing
Natalie	Doesn't let me shine
	Complains too much

Now replace the names in the first column with "I." Here is your list of "stuff" to be healed. This list indicates your disowned parts that you will work with while you read this book. The judgments you have about the difficult people in your life provide a mirror for your own self-criticism and disowned parts.

After you prepare this list, take a close look at the characteristics you have listed. How do they apply to you? Are the characteristics aimed at others or at you, or perhaps at both? For example, are you overly critical of others and of yourself? If so, why? Do your best to determine not only how these characteristics apply to you but also how they may have developed so that you may work through them, healing both yourself and your relationships with others. For example, when was the first time you can remember being critical? What was the first criticism you can remember receiving? Who was being critical? How did you feel about it? Look for examples from your past to help account for traits in yourself, especially those you have difficulty accepting as being part of you.

4

MEETING THE INNER LION

To him who is in fear, everything rustles.
—Sophocles, *Acrisius*

I have seen the enemy, and he is us.
—Pogo (Walt Kelley)

How much pain have cost us the evils
which have never happened!
—Thomas Jefferson, *A Decalogue of Canons*
for Observation in Practical Life

*J*ust as lion tamers must understand the wild animals that they work alongside, so, too, must they understand themselves. In the dangerous world of lion taming, a lack of confidence or a lack of control can expose the lion tamer to attack. The lion tamer must understand her own limits in these areas and work to go beyond them by learning what it is within her that might hold her back. She must uncover and appreciate her buried fears and doubts and other negative emotions that might rise up in her in certain stressful situations, hindering her ability to control the animals. The next step in our discussion of lion taming, then, is learning to identify what I call your "stuff"—that scared, angry, frustrated, or hopeless feeling that appears in your body during an encounter with a difficult person. In learning about your "stuff"—learning how to identify it, where it originates, and how to take control of it—you become able to separate it from the situations in which these feelings arise, giving yourself the ability to identify and ease the fear underlying the conflict rather than feed it.

In this chapter, you will learn how to take responsibility for your bag of "stuff." We all have one. Although it is triggered in the present, its origins are in the past, when it was first created by childhood hurts. As you have grown, so has your bag of "stuff," which has expanded to include denied parts of yourself. When we don't take responsibility for our "stuff," it feeds current resentments and appears in our judgments of others. As I described in the previous chapter, we can find out what needs to be healed in us by examining these judgments. The exercises at the end of this chapter encourage you to examine your own "stuff" closely by introducing you to how your "stuff" manifests as a physical sensation in your body and providing an effective method to work your way through it.

It's a Jungle in There

Within you is a collection of unruly animals wreaking havoc with your relationships. They roar, growl, and pounce. They fly up to the ceiling and drop things on others. They sneak, slither, and bite. I refer to them collectively as your "stuff." "Stuff" has two parts, a past and a present. The past is what happened to you while you were growing up. It is beliefs that you formed through your early experiences and beliefs that you took on from your family and friends. The present is how that past of yours is affecting you at this very moment. It is the physiology in our bodies during an event, followed by our behavior. It is a tightness in the chest, butterflies in the stomach, a rush of adrenaline in the bloodstream. "Stuff" is fear, fed by childhood memories of trauma and loss, and emotional wounds manifesting in current resentments, worries, and frustrations. It is sometimes as much physical as emotional, as in the case of genetically inherited depression or fluctuating blood sugar, for example. The behavior component is yelling, blaming, complaining, speaking calmly, doing nothing, overspending, withdrawing, lying, punching someone, eating twelve Ho-Ho's, drinking a pint of Jack Daniel's. It is reacting in a way that you believe to be somewhat, if not completely, out of your present control, and it almost always leads to greater conflict with others.

Why am I talking about our "stuff" when what you want to know is what to do about those difficult people out there? I have one excellent and simple reason: Unlike the behavior of others, you have direct control over your "stuff," and the more you heal in yourself, the less difficulty you will have with others. (I discuss this healing process further in Chapters 5 and 6.) The fact is, you probably aren't aware how often you are being difficult with others. You're the "nice" one, right? You may sound polite while the other rages, but underneath, your physiology boils and flops. You judge that you are the one who is "right" and that the person being difficult is "wrong." You think to yourself, or even say out loud to others, "I would never do anything like that." Have you seen what you look like in situations like this? It's not a pretty sight. When I'm being nice and am confident that I am right, my own face takes on a set look. My mouth may be smiling, but my smile is pinched and there is no friendliness in my eyes. Inside, I am judging and blaming.

Before my interest led me to learn about dealing with difficult people, I had few responses to criticism or hostile aggression: fear, sadness, defensiveness, anger, self-righteousness, and self-pity. Now that I know that each of us is either in a state of some form of fear or in a state of some form of love, I'm much less likely to take criticism or aggression personally. Even at age thirteen, I sensed that people sometimes reacted in ways that were inexplicable to me and obviously unrelated to what I had done. One friend became enraged during a PE class because I tapped her on the cheek. We had been kidding around, laughing, but suddenly, after I touched her cheek, she scolded, "Don't ever do that again!" Even with no training or formal education, I knew that she was reacting to something that had happened earlier. Knowing this, I could say, "Sorry." (I learned later that the meaning of our communication is the response we elicit. What I mean is that we must take responsibility for what we said if the person receiving our message misunderstands our intention. It is our responsibility to clear up any misunderstandings. Regarding the situation in the PE class, I later found out that my friend had been slapped across the face regularly by her alcoholic mother.)

A Look into Three Bags of "Stuff"

The following examples demonstrate different ways that people act when in the presence of the physiology that I'm calling their "stuff."

Twenty-six-year-old Susan gave up her baby for adoption after a long soul search. She had no job, lived with her mother in a condominium, and did not feel emotionally mature enough to raise a child. The father of her child was absent. Her decision was a difficult one, but she did not regret her choice. To soothe herself, she got a puppy, a golden Labrador retriever. Although she loved the dog, it chewed up her only tennis shoes and kept her awake at night, whining and wanting to play. When she went looking for a job, the dog barked and cried for hours. Two weeks after the dog's arrival, she answered the doorbell to find her landlord standing there with an angry, tense look on his face. The puppy greeted him by jumping enthusiastically on his leg. "No dogs!" he said roughly. "Get rid of it."

Susan felt a rage boil up from deep inside of her. "I will not get rid of my dog! He doesn't chew things, and he's housebroken. He won't hurt anything." The landlord was unmoved by both her anger and tears. "No dogs. I'll give you until the weekend to get the dog out of my condo."

Susan's mother returned from work that evening to find her sobbing. After Susan explained the situation, her mother tried to comfort her, but Susan was inconsolable. The doorbell rang and again the landlord appeared, this time more upset than before. "Your daughter left hateful messages on my answering machine, filled with profanity. I will not allow her to occupy my living quarters. Both she and the dog have to be out of here by the weekend."

In this example, Susan's "stuff" appeared to her to be about the dog. But, as she discovered later, it really was related to unexpressed grief about giving up her child. She ended up moving in with a friend and getting a job, but she did not keep the dog even though she could have in her new quarters. She gave it to her older sister to raise. Her own (internal) conflict about the time, expense, and attention a small puppy took was projected onto her (external) landlord. Her anger at the landlord represented her pattern of blaming others, which she could learn only in hindsight. At the time, she was convinced that she was a victim of her circumstances even though she was making the choices that created her life.

In the next example, a man's anger blinds him to the fact that something important is going on inside of him. He mistakenly believes that his anger is caused by the external events that are occurring.

It was a freezing, rainy night when the heavy, balding businessman opened his car door. As he made his way toward his luxury home, his wing tips splashed in the puddles, soaking his socks. "Damn!" he said. He felt the blood rise up his neck, and his head throbbed. That evening, his only child, Noreen, and her husband visited with their two rambunctious offspring, and in their playfulness, the children knocked his favorite lamp to the floor, breaking it. "That does it!" he yelled at his daughter. "Can't you control your children?" His face was red, but his eyes looked weary and scared.

The next week, in one of my classes, he expressed his regret over the argument with his daughter. His regret was not just for this single incident. Because it was obvious to him that in this case his daughter (and her children) were not to blame for how he felt, he remembered other times when he had viewed her as a difficult person. For the past forty years, he had worked long days and believed it was natural to feel drained and empty when he returned home. Often, when he needed time to himself, his extroverted daughter wanted someone to listen to her newfound opinions. These opposing needs resulted in misunderstanding.

At first, he was sure that the way he felt was directly related to his grandchildren's behavior and the "poor parenting" his daughter was providing. Afterward and during class, however, he realized that it was, in fact, his "stuff" that was the source of his pain. His impending retirement brought new fears that unsettled old grief, upsetting him. In addition to past regrets, he uncovered fears about aging, having "time run out," and how his new life would be.

This man had been taught early on to keep his pain bottled up. He had stored grief from the past and hid his fear about the future. The source of the argument was his fear. It's a choice, a habit, to take one's fear and turn it onto others—but habits can be broken. He spent the next three weeks feeling like an emotional wreck, releasing swallowed tears and anger in class and facing his own mortality. Instead of running from the blank screen of his life ahead of him, he began to brainstorm ideas for his future. As he accepted his negative feelings, he began to feel free and light. In his own way, he made amends to his daughter by inviting her for dinner and never mentioning the incident. As a class assignment, he wrote the following letter and submitted it to me:

Dear Noreen,

> *Lately, I've been reflecting on my life, and I realize that when I am upset about something, I take it out on others. I used to think the feeling of stress in my body was caused by what was happening around me. So when I got an angry feeling, I would find someone or something to blame. There was always something going on that I could believe was the reason for my stress. I apologize for my behavior when you visited. What could have been a time of love became a battlefield because I took out my anger on you.*
>
> *You are important to me, and I'm proud of you. You are loving with your children in a way I was never able to be with you. I did not express the love I felt for you, but I want you to know now how much I love you.*
>
> *Now that I'm retiring, I realize I gave my best to my work life and the leftovers to you. My job won't be there anymore. I've already been replaced. But you will be there. The lamp*

that broke will not be needed. Any other can provide light to read by. But you are irreplaceable. There is no one exactly like you. No one lights up the room with their smile like you do. No one looks to me for guidance, then rejects it and does the opposite. No one else calls me "Dad."

Please forgive me for any pain I have caused you. I am learning to be more human.

Love,
Dad

Ideally, he would have spoken these words to his daughter or given her a copy of the letter, but he did not. Still, he saw great improvement in his relationship with her. Although many of the letters written in my class are not passed along to the people they were written to, many of the relationships still improve because of the healing that occurs in the letter writers as they take the time to explore and express their feelings about the conflict. When fear in its many forms is accepted and released, the love that was there all along is uncovered.

In the next example, we can see how someone can be so caught up in her own fears that she imagines a rejection that never occurs.

Janine, a small business owner, submitted a proposal to Jeff, the president of a large department store chain. She writes about how she calls up her "stuff" through her negative thought process.

Two weeks after submitting my proposal, I ran into Jeff at a social event. I was full of anticipation about finding out what his opinion was. Naturally, I hoped he had liked it. When he saw me, he said hello and asked how I was. We chatted about the party and the hostess, who is a mutual friend. I returned to my seat next to my husband and began a familiar process of creating an internal feeling of stress. He hates it, I thought to myself as I made feeble attempts at conversation with the people at our table. That's why he didn't say anything. I felt a sinking feeling in my stomach.

For the next twenty minutes or so, I sifted through my thoughts of failure: Great! You quit your steady job, you dope, to start this business, and now it's not working out! What made you think you could do it? You had a perfectly good job. What an idiot! The more I thought about it, the worse I felt. I felt so nauseated from all the fear I was creating that I considered quietly calling a cab and going home. I couldn't tell my husband, though, because that might attract attention from others at our table to what I was feeling inside. I was sure that my life was doomed. At the end of the evening, I found out that Jeff hadn't even read the proposal yet! I had created all that stress over nothing. When he did finally read it, he loved it.

Although these examples illustrate different people feeling different emotions, the message is the same for all: How you feel is separate from the circumstances around you. How you feel and what your physiology registers are largely determined by your perception, by what you make of what you see, feel, hear, taste, and smell, and by your response to influence from your family, culture, and work setting. How you feel is determined by these perceptions and by how much of your own "stuff" needs to be examined through the cleansing fire of consciousness.

The Conspiracy of Emotion

We are part of a culture that has decided not only what is good and what is bad but also how we're supposed to feel. Subtly and persistently, it instructs us to feel good in the presence of certain conditions and bad in the presence of others. Apart from that conditioning, the reaction of the "stuff" for each of us doesn't depend on the circumstance.

We don't need to buy into the notion that certain things make us feel bad. How we feel is determined by what we think about and say to ourselves about our lives.

The way you perceive the events in your life is your choice. When you feel miserable, it is not the fault of someone or some event. Feeling miserable is the result of a habit of negative thought patterns. You will find acceptance in the world for the notion that certain things, like working with difficult people, for example, cause stress. Don't buy into it! Find out for yourself that the people "out there" are a reflection of your conflict inside. Feeling miserable is the result of that bag of unhealed "stuff."

Getting to Know Your "Stuff"

You probably will never know the contents of the difficult person's bag of "stuff." All you need to know is that what you are dealing with is his pain and suffering. You can, however, discover the contents of your own bag of "stuff." Perhaps you are not speaking your truth because you've developed a habit of "not making waves" and stifling your ideas. Perhaps you learned as a child by observing the behavior of your family, that expressing anger is wrong or, conversely, that expressing anger is the only way to get results. Perhaps you're in the wrong job. Maybe you've wanted to try your hand at something new but are afraid to leave your comfort zone, so your stress level increases, but you still blame others for how you feel. Perhaps you are torn because part of you believes that your career is your higher priority, while another part of you believes that you are not spending enough time with your children. Perhaps you're neglecting your creative side or some special ability you have. Were you once a person who loved to draw, paint, make things with your hands, sing, play an instrument, cook a meal, write? Perhaps you have traded that fire in your eye for a paycheck. The money and perks are so good that you can't bear to leave your position at work even if you are bored with the sameness of your job. Perhaps you're living somebody else's life. Maybe your parents had a plan for you from the start and you obligingly followed it even though it was never your plan. Perhaps you're spending too much time trying to get instead of giving. If you have the belief that you're running out of time or money, you might find yourself hoarding both.

We all share the loss of love and friendship, suffer from self-doubt and "failures," retain grudges, childhood wounds, and old beliefs, and grow old. To deal with such pain is to face it, experience it, accept it into your heart, put it into perspective, and release it. When you don't deal with it—that is, you send it inward, denied—then, as the years go by and you're faced with something, like a pesky salesman or a mistake on your telephone bill, you have little or no flexibility to deal with the "stuff" because it's been accumulating as you have been running from it.

There are three phases to becoming acquainted with your "stuff":

＊ Recognizing how your "stuff" comes up as a physical response in your life now
＊ Examining what you do when you feel that response
＊ Identifying old hurts buried from past events

Getting control is like developing any new skill. First, you become aware of where you are now, not where you think you are, but what you would see if you could somehow follow yourself around objectively for a week. (Most people think that they are good at communicating and that those they consider difficult are not, but we all have room for improvement.) After you become aware of how your "stuff" functions, the next step is to bring that awareness to your consciousness while you are experiencing the effects of your "stuff" and then to acknowledge to yourself, "This is mine."

To begin the process, concentrate on identifying situations that evoke a stress response, notice how you handle your stress, and use this information to trace your reaction back to the time when you formed the physical response. Even though the past experience came first, you will have greater success if you start with your experience in the present and then trace the experience back. We often bury the memory in our attempt to get rid of the unpleasant feeling. An explanation of the three phases follows. I also have included exercises at the end of this chapter to assist you in recognizing when you're suffering the effects of your "stuff."

Phase 1: Recognizing the Sensation of Your "Stuff"

You may notice that you become overly resentful when you are told what to do and how to do it. Your "stuff" may appear in comments such as "I want to do things my way" and conflict with authority figures. Perhaps, when you are told how to write reports or what the highest priority at work should be, you feel an urge to rebel. The physical experience might be a feeling of alarm, the sensation you would feel if you were under attack. The sensation might begin in your head, as heat, and then travel throughout your body.

A second person in this same situation might feel afraid when told how to do something. This person might worry about getting it right or wonder if the reason he is being given specific instructions is that he has not been performing well. This reaction might lead to a quivering sensation in the stomach.

Phase 2: Examining What You Do When You Feel That Response

You might then begin to defend yourself (also known as blaming). You might notice you become easily irritated and snap at others.

The second person in our example might shrink back or turn his feelings inward. He might spend much of his day in silence.

Keep a record of your encounters with your "stuff." Write down how it feels when you sense the presence of your "stuff" and what you do during those times, immediately afterward, ten minutes later, and an hour later.

Phase 3: Identifying Old Hurts

One woman in class, who identified herself as a difficult person, traced her current problem of butting into others' conversations and trying to get herself invited to events back to a third grade incident.

She remembered that she had not been invited to a birthday party that included several friends from her class. She reexperienced the hurt she had felt originally at being excluded. It was during that original experience that she formed the belief that she was not important.

Here is another example that represents an early incident that contributed to creating "stuff" about authority figures:

My earliest memory of stress with a difficult person occurred at Golden Gate Park in San Francisco, where a man posed as a policeman when a friend and I were innocently playing. I knew no boundaries then. To me, a park was for everyone; a place to rejoice in being alive. It contained so many possibilities: swings, a merry-go-round, flowers, the Japanese Tea Garden, the band concert on Sunday afternoons.

I was eight-years-old and had taken my bicycle for a day of exploring in San Francisco with my friend, Alan. We had baloney sandwiches, an apple, a handful of Mint Julep candies, and a thermos of milk between us. A garden area in the botanical gardens was divided by a small stream. We stopped to splash in the water, removed our shoes, rolled up our jeans, and watched life forms in the water, fascinated. Little frogs in various stages delighted us: We observed pollywogs and others that looked like fish with buds. The day was clear and warm, and the scent of fresh air treated our nostrils. Seated on the bank, surrounded by beautiful flowers, Alan and I ate our lunches, our feet dangling in the cool stream. Our eyes were shining. We were completely present in the moment, happy to be alive.

After lunch, we returned to explore the water. Dozens of little frogs hopped around, providing a game of chase. I caught one, cupping it in my small hand, thrilling to the tickle of its legs in my palm. Giggling, I dropped it back into the water. Suddenly, a huge man appeared and thundered: "You're under arrest!" He was furious. "Don't you know it's against the law to be in here?" He didn't look like a policeman, but he talked as if he were one. Neither of us said a word. We stepped out of the stream, reaching for our socks, while he continued to shame us, bellowing, "How dare you! I am going to have you locked up for good." My body filled with the queasy feeling of shame.

This was a powerful incident that formed a faulty belief I carry to this day about making mistakes: When someone is angry, it means I have done something wrong. The way it shows up today is if any person in an authority position gives me a direction that I think is rude, I react in one of two ways: One way is to feel shame, as if I've done something terrible. It begins in my stomach as a scared feeling, then travels up my spine, enclosing my head with a hot, quavery sensation. The second way of responding is to quickly shift the shame feeling to anger, as if I'm being attacked and need to fight for my life. This is a more powerful feeling and preferable to the first response. It's as if I'm acting like the mean man in the park. "How dare you treat me like that!" this feeling says. The trouble with this reaction is that I burn a lot of bridges when I react this way. And when I look back later, I realize that I was making a big deal out of some little thing. It's like removing a splinter with a hacksaw. Sure, the sliver is gone, but so is the finger!

As you become a tamer of lions, you learn what needs attention within yourself. In fact, you cannot do one without doing the other. All the elements of lion taming that I discuss in this book are interrelated. As you build skills and gain confidence in one area, you do so in other areas also. People will notice that you do not remain the target of a person's rage, but they might not know what it is you are doing differently because the skills that you will be using—expanding your comfort zone, removing characterizations, and taking responsibility for your own "stuff"—will have gradually become part of your personality.

After you have gotten to know your "stuff" and you've indicated whether you tend to project it more onto others or turn it in on *yourself (or both), the next step is to heal it. Now that you are beginning the process of taking responsibility for your "stuff," you are ready to move into the next chapter, in which you will learn how to heal it as it comes up.*

Exercise 1: Meeting Your "Stuff" in the Present

The following is an exercise to introduce you to how your "stuff" feels when you experience it. Write at the top of a piece of paper or in your notebook, "This is my 'stuff.' It is independent from what is going on. I am responsible for this." Recognizing your "stuff" as it comes up is the first step toward healing it. The questions are intended to help you form a vivid image in your mind that has form and color. This process helps you to get the feeling outside of yourself so that you gain greater objectivity about it and thus more control. Then when you have the sensation, you can remember, "Aha! This is my 'stuff;' a lion, a dragon, fear, anger."

1. Think of a time when you had an unpleasant interaction with someone; a time when you did not like how you felt and how you handled yourself. When you have picked a specific instance, give it a name, such as "Stuff," "Fear," or "Anger," and write it down on your page.
2. Where is the feeling located in your body when it starts?
3. Is the feeling soft or hard, and does it move or stay in one place?
4. What color would you assign to this feeling?
5. If this feeling were an animal or a human, what form would it take?
6. Draw a representation of this feeling.

Now think of a time when you experienced what might represent the opposite of this feeling; a time when you felt wonderful. When you have a specific time in mind, respond to the following six items. On a separate piece of paper or in your notebook, write a heading such as "This Is How I Feel Without My 'Stuff,'" "Love," or "Peace." Then respond to the following:

1. Write down the name of this feeling.
2. Where is the feeling located in your body when it starts?
3. Is the feeling soft or hard, and does it move or stay in one place?
4. What color would you assign to this feeling?
5. If this feeling were animal or human, what form would it take?
6. Draw a representation of this feeling.

Now imagine yourself going through the difficult experience with the good feeling, even though it did not happen this way originally. Just watch what happens in your imagination when you visualize the experience with this other feeling. If the sequence of events changes, let it change. You might find yourself in your visualization handling the situation better than you originally did. You also might find others responding differently to you because of how you are now.

Important: This exercise is not intended to point out that you acted wrongly during the unpleasant interaction. At each moment, we do the best with what we know at the time. Resist the temptation to criticize your behavior. Instead, acknowledge to yourself that you are now able to respond in both ways if you need to. Learning an alternative response does not mean that the initial one was wrong. You are adding to your already perfect self.

Exercise 2: What I Do When in My "Stuff"

When in the presence of my "stuff" I tend to
- Withdraw   1_____ 2_____ 3_____ 4_____ 5_____
                 least likely   most likely

- Turn it inward on myself as criticism
           1_____ 2_____ 3_____ 4_____ 5_____
                 least likely   most likely

- Blame it on others
           1_____ 2_____ 3_____ 4_____ 5_____
                 least likely   most likely

Exercise 3: Finding the Incident from Your Past and Then Reframing It

Go back to Exercise 1, in which you identified your "stuff," and again let that feeling return to your body. Let it be present for a moment while your eyes are closed. Now, as you pay attention to the feeling and notice where it is located in your body, remember another time when you felt this way. Preferably, remember a time when you were quite young. Give this memory a title, such as "Mean Man in Park" or "Fight on the Playground." When you have selected a particular incident, identify what you needed to have then that you didn't—such as information, courage, muscle, a protective adult, or the right words—and imagine your adult self being in the picture coaching your younger self. In your mind, imagine your adult self giving your child self whatever was needed. Imagine a conversation with your younger self in which your adult self tells your child self what you needed to hear at that earlier age. Now imagine your younger self going through the same incident but with the added resources.

For those of you who have difficulty visualizing, use a photo-graph, a stuffed animal, or another object to represent your younger self and go through the same process above.

5

HEALING THE INNER LION

Hungry? Eat.
Tired? Sleep.
Sad? Cry.

—Claudio Albarran[1]

Everyone carries a shadow, and the less it is embodied
in the individual's conscious life, the blacker and denser it is.
At all counts, it forms an unconscious snag, thwarting
our most well-meant intentions.

—Carl G. Jung[2]

As you forgive him, you restore to truth
what was denied by both of you.

—*A Course in Miracles*[3]

[On forgiveness] This little step, so small
it has escaped your notice, is a stride through time
into eternity, beyond all ugliness into beauty
that will enchant you, and will never cease to
cause you wonderment at its perfection.

—*A Course in Miracles*[4]

A thankful person is thankful under all circumstances.
A complaining soul complains even if he lives in paradise.

—Bahá'u'lláh, quoted in *A Grateful Heart: Daily Blessings*
for the Evening Meal from Buddha to the Beatles

A lion tamer having a bad day does not take it out on the animals. If she did, she would be met with sound and fury—the lions instinctively would respond in kind. Instead, the lion tamer is respectful of the beasts and learns to clear herself of stress and unfinished business before she enters the ring. Long ago, she discovered that possessing knowledge about the animals and the skills required to guide them is not enough. Control over the animals requires control over herself. To face the challenges awaiting her in the ring, she must first face the challenges within herself. She must determine what her primary sources of stress and conflict are and deal with them so that she can meet the wild animals awaiting her in the ring feeling alert and confident.

The skills you are learning will increase your confidence when faced with the lions in your life. Because our "stuff" at times interferes with our feeling of confidence, the next step is to diminish it. In Chapter 4, you learned how to identify the presence of "stuff" in your life. This chapter focuses on healing it—on your ability to choose your attitude, on ways to heal your emotional pain, and on the importance of forgiveness. By engaging in the healing process described below, and by forgiving those who have harmed you, you diminish your bag of "stuff," leaving yourself in a better state to be in the presence of lions.

Choosing Your Positive Attitude

In Chapter 1, I discussed the importance of selecting a positive outlook in dealing with difficult people. In no aspect of dealing with your lions is a positive attitude more important than in healing the "stuff" that interferes with your relationships with others. The knowledge that you have the power to choose your own attitude will help you through those times when you want to run from your pain or blame it on others rather than heal it. Like most people, you may believe that your attitude is simply a reflection of what is happening around you, something automatic and outside of your control. It is not. A "bad attitude" has less to do with traffic jams and frustration at work than it does unhealed "stuff." Negative attitudes reflect inner fear. We experience ourselves from the inside out. Others experience only the external manifestation of our inner struggle. If we have internal pain and inner conflict, they manifest as a negative attitude.

The words in the Stan Wells song "The Mirror"[5] describe how the world reflects our attitude rather than the other way around:

I've noticed that when I am feeling so high
Everybody seems to shine,
Everybody seems to me to shine.
And whenever I'm low I guess I could say,
Everything all around me looks gray,
Everything all around me looks gray.
Cause all that I do,
All that I see
Is really a perfect reflection of me.

So if the world all around you looks gloomy today,
Take a look right inside your own door,
A look right inside your own door.
Open your heart and your mind
And the love that's there inside,
Will spread from you to the world evermore,
From you to the world evermore.

Cause all that you see,
And all that you do
Is really a perfect reflection of you.

We choose the attitude with which we face the day. In the movie *It's a Wonderful Life*, George Bailey, played by James Stewart, grows increasingly unhappy because he believes he cannot adequately support his family and because he resents the daily struggles he must endure as president of the small local building and loan. After discovering that $8,000 of the funds belonging to the building and loan has been misplaced, he finally decides that he has had enough. He decides to jump off a bridge into the icy river below to end his life. An angel in a human body intervenes, showing him what the world would have been like if he had never lived. Shifting his focus from what is wrong with his life to the contributions he has made and to his loving circle of family and friends, Bailey is once more happy to be alive. Rushing into his home to be reunited with his wife and children at the end of the film, he finds a man waiting to arrest him for the loss of the money. "Isn't that wonderful?" Bailey asks enthusiastically. "I'm going to jail!" His circumstances have not changed, but his attitude has.

Of course, *It's a Wonderful Life* is only a movie. As shown in that film, however, we often require a crisis in our own lives to waken us to the awareness that we choose our attitude just as we choose what to wear each day. Because our reactions happen so rapidly and unconsciously, however, it's easy to form habits that are difficult to break and then believe they are a necessary part of us. If you have lived a life habitually worrying, negatively judging others, and wishing that those people were out of your life, you may think it impossible to live any other way. Many of us feel justified in pointing the finger of blame at others.

Instead, you can choose to see the difficult people in your life as teachers with important lessons for you about yourself. When a difficult person enters your life, encourage yourself to be curious about what the experience might teach you. Step back far enough from your emotional involvement in the situation to observe it as if you were watching a movie. The reward for recognizing that you choose your attitude in your interactions with difficult people is the knowledge you obtain about yourself and the peace you bring to your relationships.

The Healing Process

As I discussed in Chapter 4, the presence of a difficult person in your life is an indication of the need for healing in you. After you have identified this need in yourself, you will no doubt want to remove the pain from your life and move on to greater happiness and more fulfilling relationships with others. Dr. Susan Trout, in her book *To See Differently*, describes the process for healing emotional wounds.[6] According to Trout, the healing process involves the following elements:

- ❧ Shedding swallowed tears
- ❧ Delivering undelivered communications
- ❧ Releasing suppressed negative emotions
- ❧ Owning all parts of yourself

Shedding Swallowed Tears

Grief is cumulative. If you have suffered losses (and life, despite its wonders and joys, is a series of losses) but did not allow yourself to sufficiently grieve and weep, those tears remain inside, waiting for you, until you find an avenue to express them. You might know their presence by a chronic, low-grade irritability or by long-standing depression. You might not even be aware of them until your own weeping catches you by surprise. A sad movie, a heart-felt message, a "bad day," or a difficult person might be the catalyst to bring up the swallowed sadness. The tears wash away the grief. In the following example, an estranged couple's argument brings up swallowed grief for the therapist conducting the interview. As shown in the example, sometimes addressing the conflict in other people's lives releases something in ourselves.

Janice, a counselor, met with Linda and Richard, an estranged couple. Their son, Justin, had been setting fires and engaging in other episodes of acting-out at school. Janice had heard from Linda about battles that Justin had witnessed between Linda and Richard over custody, visitation, and money. Janice had invited both parents in to meet with her in the hope that she could open the lines of communication between the two, allowing Linda and Richard to become a team united in the best interest of their son. During the meeting, the communication between the couple was tense at first and became increasingly critical and harsh. Linda said that Justin complained about being questioned by his father for information about his mother that could be used in court. At one point during the meeting, Richard told Linda that she was disgusting because she couldn't control Justin and earned no income. He ended his tirade by saying, "You're an incompetent, worthless slob."

Janice's sadness arose when she recognized that each of these individuals was in pain and calling for help. Yet both were heaping more pain on each other. How could they do that? she wondered. Don't they see how much the other is hurting? It dawned on her that in her own battle with her husband that ended in divorce years before, perhaps her husband had been in as much pain as Richard. At the time, she had been aware only of her own pain. She had believed that her husband had caused it, and she remembered wondering how he could be so insensitive. She now realized that she too, had been insensitive, and that her earlier behavior was being mirrored back to her through this couple.

As Janice became aware of her own sadness, Richard said to his former wife, "Justin never hit me or my wife until this last visit. I know he hits you all the time, and now it's showing up at my house!" Janice knew that often when there's acting-out behavior, it shows up first where the child is more comfortable to be himself, then erupts in all areas of the child's life. At other times, the behavior occurs where the child feels the most stress. Adding further stress to the environment by blaming each other is the last thing that parents should do, yet that is exactly what typically occurs in such situations. That is clearly what Janice was witnessing as the two aimed their fear for Justin blindly outward. Richard's face contorted with rage as he spoke, reddened from the adrenaline rush. Janice recognized Richard's pain and knew that it wasn't the fault of his estranged spouse. She knew Linda's pain was not Richard's fault, and she felt her own helplessness. There seemed to be no chink in the thick armor of misunderstanding. As is usually the case, both were unaware of their own contribution to the conflict. They were doing the best they could with what they knew.

The idea came to Janice to have the two parents pretend that they were meeting thirty years later, after the situation had turned out ideally for everyone involved. After she suggested the idea, Richard stood up and declared that he had had enough. "I was led to believe something different," he said. He had come to the meeting to discuss his son, and he believed that Justin's behavior was unrelated to the conflict between Linda and himself. "This game of pretend doesn't have anything to do with my son," he declared. He did not want to address his conflict with Linda because a court date to begin divorce proceedings was already scheduled, and his lawyer had instructed him not to talk to anyone about matters related to the divorce. When the discussion appeared to him to be marriage counseling, he decided that he had been deceived and stormed out of the room. Linda remained with Janice after Richard left and continued to relate stories that presented Richard as the cause of the conflict.

The counselor felt deeply saddened at the way the two parents had attacked one another and emphasized each other's mistakes and shortcomings. Linda's attacks focused on money and Richard's focused on anger. "I don't understand why you wouldn't want your son to live comfortably!" she had said to him. "Do you want him to live in a shelter?" Their words to each other had been delivered like blows, with no consideration of the damage they would leave behind.

Janice felt deep in a well of her own grief and wanted to be by herself to cry. She thought to herself, surely my own divorce had been more civilized and less angry, intense, and damaging. But then she remembered the hate and pain she had felt. Memories of hurtful things she had said and done returned to her. She could see herself in this couple. Janice put her own emotions aside by acknowledging their presence and made a promise to herself to deal with them later.

She allowed herself the hope that the difficult session could, like the painful lancing of a boil, lead to healing. She said to Linda, "It's possible that this will still have a positive outcome for your son."

To recover herself, she called a friend that night and spoke freely about her feelings, not attempting to hide her sorrow. She continued to shed swallowed tears, healing old grief from the dissolution of her marriage twenty years previously. She had been unaware of that grief's presence. She thought that she was to be the teacher and the parents the students, but today it was the other way around. Once more, she was reminded that we all take turns being students and teachers.

The difference in Janice's interactions with her ex-husband after that day was significant. They already had made peace and were polite and respectful to each other. Previously, though, she had held back parts of herself that she thought might leave her open for his judgment, such as her different attitude on raising children. For example, she had made an encouraging remark to their son about the D he had earned in a science class. "It looks like you're disappointed," she had said breezily with a smile. "Knowing you, you'll be able to pull this up." She knew that her former spouse would have wanted her to give the boy some kind of punishment for such a grade. They used to argue about their differing views, and she learned to avoid topics on which she knew they held opposing attitudes. After the grieving, she no longer felt the need to hold back. She began to volunteer stories of incidents such as this one. Disagreement no longer represented a threat to her. She found that her perspective, presented in this manner rather than in the volatile air of a heated argument, was accepted by her former husband.

The shedding of tears and the accompanying buried sadness brings freedom and release. By feeling the hurt and releasing it through tears, you are free to live without the pain.

Delivering Undelivered Communications

If you were taught not to be open about your anger and to avoid conflict, you have not learned how to assert yourself naturally. Ideally, when an issue first comes up, you speak your perspective. If you do not, what may once have been a trivial issue becomes buried and begins to swell in you like an infection that eventually shows as a lump beneath your skin. Gradually, your "stuff" appears in your life, and you feel that something is wrong even though you can't identify what it is. You may find yourself overreacting, perhaps becoming involved in a full-blown fight. If you make the effort to determine the real source of the fight, you'll find that incident, or perhaps a pattern in your behavior, that you had buried earlier. As you participate in the healing process, you find that delivering your truth requires no special effort when your pain is gone. Our most natural state is love, but our "stuff" sometimes covers it with anxiety and anger.

How much of your truth can you deliver? How far out of your comfort zone are you willing to venture? In the following example, a couple argues about whether to spend the weekend together or to do chores separately. The argument brings up undelivered communications. Both had fears about spending a long stretch of time apart, but neither was willing to share the truth with the other.

A happily married couple, Julie and Sam had enjoyed a week of bliss in their lakefront home, when, gradually, tension began to arise. Julie had witnessed the increasing tension and wariness in Sam and thought that he was causing the estrangement. Sam had observed a coolness in Julie and thought that she was upset because he was going to be traveling alone in Hawaii for three months to celebrate his recent retirement. When he observed that she wasn't talking about it, he decided that he wouldn't either.

While they were walking their dogs around the lake on the Saturday morning before the Monday Sam was due to leave for Hawaii, Julie initiated a conversation. "I realize I'm mad because you're leaving for so long. I thought we would at least spend today together."

"Why didn't you say something before?" Sam asked, frustrated. "I have left important things I need to do before I leave. I have just one day to pay bills and do my taxes."

"I didn't know it was bothering me that much," she admitted.

He replied, "Well, I've been talking about this for over a year, and you never said anything. You encouraged me to do this."

"I thought you wouldn't go for so long," she said. "I had it in my mind that you would change it to one month, since we've been married for only eight months. I thought you would know what I've been thinking. I thought you would say, 'I don't want to be gone from you for that long.'"

He asked her, "How was I supposed to know it when you weren't saying anything?"

Feeling foolish, she said, "Well, I didn't want to have to ask you to be with me. I wanted you to want it. I guess I expected you to read my mind."

"And I've been avoiding you because I'm afraid to be without you for so long, but this isn't how I want to be feeling." Sam was calmer now, and sadder.

The argument was a distraction from the fear they both felt about the separation. Julie's fear was about being without Sam, and Sam's fear was about separation from his life-long work, being away from Julie, and acknowledging his impending old age. In a way, Sam felt worse when the argument was resolved, and he was again faced with his painful fears. In a kind of knee-jerk response, Sam would become angry at others when he experienced these "bad" feelings. This was his way of running from his pain. He began to pay attention to these deeper, painful fears by being still, allowing their presence, and accepting them into his heart. Then he thought about what he wanted to do with his remaining years. He resolved to address unfinished business in his life. Specifically, he wanted to forgive his late father. He decided to accomplish that forgiveness with the help of a male counselor, and he joined a men's group to deal with his anger and grief. By following this process, he avoided needless blaming (anger focused out at others) or depression (anger focused in on oneself), and he found himself much happier afterward. As you begin to ferret out your undelivered communications, you find parts of yourself that you have buried or rejected. With Sam, it was his anger and grief concerning his father.

The next example tells of a class participant, Robert, a manager for a large company, who stretched his comfort zone to deliver his truth to one of his employees. He had been worrying that Jake, one of his employees, was no longer pulling his weight on the team. Others had complained to Robert to "do something about Jake." Although Robert was uncomfortable initially because he thought he was butting in (and quietly he hoped that the situation would improve without his contribution), he finally decided to speak to Jake because he knew that he could do so with honesty and a real concern for his employee.

I knew that in six months I would have to evaluate Jake and that if things didn't improve, it would be a negative evaluation. Not only does a negative evaluation lower an employee's pay rate, but Jake was headed toward being laid off or fired due to his declining performance, and he didn't know it. I, of course, would be the one to have to break the news, and I didn't want that.

When I first knew Jake, he had always been good company because he was doing what he enjoyed. Now, whenever I saw him, he looked tired, and he complained constantly. He had been in his current position for six years, and he was tired of it. His heart was not in his work. Although he spent time at work, he did only what was necessary and didn't look beyond that. He thought that he was a victim, that life was too hard, and that others were the cause of his distress.

I asked him about the rest of his life and learned that it matched his work: He went through the motions, complained a lot, and took no action to improve anything. He had neither interest nor optimism in any area of his life.

It wasn't always this way. Previously, Jake performed at a high level, was enthusiastic, and was passionate about scuba diving. I believed that it could be that way for him again. Although it was hard for me to get started, I called him into my office and told him that I thought he was depressed to such a level that it was negatively affecting his life. I told him the facts about his work status. I suggested that he get an evaluation to rule out possible clinical depression.

Jake wasn't surprised at what I said, and it gave him the motivation to do something about his condition. He made a series of appointments and eventually was placed on a tempo-

rary regimen of antidepressant medication. He was told that the medication would give him some time out from being immobilized so he could get his life back on track. After approximately six weeks, Jake changed jobs, and when I see him now, he looks happy.

In the previous examples, we saw how delivering undelivered communications dramatically improved the lives of the people involved. Direct communication—that is, communication delivered when the situation first arises—prevents messages from being undelivered in the first place and thus avoids later conflict. Although communicating directly may not always have an immediate positive outcome, the benefit for you is immeasurable as you develop the habit of accepting all parts of yourself and speaking directly to others from that truth. When you've chosen an attitude of acceptance for yourself and others and you take responsibility for and heal your "stuff," what you say is firm and doesn't cause conflict. On the other hand, when you speak from a blaming attitude or while you're lost in the effect of your "stuff," then you add to the fear. Review the simple, direct exchanges that follow. Note that the responses are both straightforward and respectful.

- ❖ "Please come to my party tonight." "Thank you for including me, but I need to have time alone right now."
- ❖ "Here, have a drink." "No, thank you." "Oh, come on. I have something you would like." "No, thank you."
- ❖ "Why don't you just snap out of it?" "I've learned to let myself grieve as long as it takes."
- ❖ "What? You're not finished with that yet?" "No, I'm not. It took more time than I expected."
- ❖ "You mean we have to reschedule the meeting?" "Yes, I need another week to prepare."

Releasing Suppressed Negative Emotions

Although the two elements may seem quite similar at first, there is a significant difference between delivering undelivered communications and releasing suppressed negative emotions. The former involves saying what you believe it is important for you to say instead of not saying anything and avoiding possible conflict. The latter involves allowing yourself to feel pain from which you've been running. Emotions suppressed in the past cannot be denied and will seek a way to become manifest in the present.

If you decided not to acknowledge when you feel "unwelcome" emotions, such as irritability, sadness, anger, hurt, envy, jealousy, or guilt, you have buried them inside you. For example, if you believe that it is wrong to feel anger, then you have accumulated angry feelings over the years that need to be released. Suppose you've recently had a loss: an important project you were working on was canceled, a relationship ended, or you got fired from a job. Through it all, you remained stoic; you never acknowledged your bad feelings about the event. Then your teenage son talks back to you, storms out of the house, and stays out much later than house rules allow. Because of your denied and buried pain, you lack the flexibility to handle the stressful events of life that inevitably come up. You perceive the trial-and-error growth episodes of others as a burden to you, rather than as steps in a necessary learning process for them with you as coach. When your son returns home, you preach and criticize, causing further separation, instead of expressing your real concern and then providing a logical consequence for the behavior, such as limiting your son's freedom until he earns it back through cooperation. Although you believe that your rage is justified, you are overlooking the fact that your overreaction is a sure sign that you need to address something within.

Jennifer, a 34-year-old bus driver, was having problems getting along with a co-worker, Mona. Although she acted angry toward Mona, she actually was afraid of her. Jennifer was unsure of her ability to defuse a potential conflict between them. The conflict originated when a set of tools disappeared between the day and night shifts. Mona worked night shift; Jennifer worked days. Jennifer believed that Mona took the tools. In hushed tones, and acknowledging that her fear sounded extreme, Jennifer confided in class that she thought Mona posed a threat to her life. She role-played how the following day at work might go, playing the role of her "difficult" colleague. A class participant took the role of Jennifer. After observing herself objectively through another person and walking a bit in Mona's shoes, Jennifer realized that her life wasn't in danger. She wondered why she felt so strongly about Mona.

Over the course of several weeks, Jennifer remembered a babysitter she had at age six, who reminded her of Mona. Her babysitter was a woman full of her own rage who took it out on her charges with yelling and spanking. One incident in particular stood out in Jennifer's memory. Jennifer had taken a toy workbench away from a younger child and had been hit repeatedly by the adult babysitter for making the boy cry. In class, she was able to express her hurt and angry feelings toward the woman. From playing the part of the babysitter, she imagined the misery that would allow the woman to become so abusive. Then she forgave her. The conflict with Mona disappeared.

Owning All Parts of Yourself

Barbara Hannah, a student of Carl Jung, describes how addressing conflict with someone can serve as a metaphor for dealing with conflict within ourselves:

> *I remember a very wise woman telling me that, on a long tour through countries she had always wanted to visit, she was forced to share a room with another woman who was completely uncongenial to her. At first she felt this would inevitably spoil the tour. Then she realized that she would waste one of the most interesting and pleasurable times of her life if she allowed her dislike to spoil it. Therefore, she set herself to accept her uncongenial companion, detaching herself*

from her negative feelings and from the woman herself, while being friendly and kind toward her. This technique worked marvelously, and she managed to enjoy the tour immensely.

It is just the same with elements from the unconscious that we dislike and which we feel are very uncongenial to us. We spoil our own tour through life if we allow ourselves to resent them. If we can accept them for what they are and be friendly toward them, we often find they are not so bad after all; and at least we are spared their hostility.[7]

Just as the woman in the tale accepted her difficult companion, so do we need to accept all parts of ourselves. By being in conflict with parts of ourselves, or shutting them out, we start an internal war that takes up quite a bit of our energy. Inevitably, the conflict builds up inside us and spills out on others as anger. As Walt Whitman said, we contain multitudes. Inside each of us, you'll find greed, anger, jealousy, lust, envy, and pettiness, as well as generosity, love, trust, gladness for others, and wisdom. To know if you have accepted all parts of yourself, look to your judgments. If the behavior of others draws particularly strong criticism from you, you can be sure that you have buried some related part of yourself.

As you discovered in the exercise at the end of Chapter 3, in coming to know the judgments you make about the difficult people in your life, you come to know unacknowledged parts of yourself. It could be a shadow side, a critic, an exploiter, a manipulator. When you buried it, you also buried its opposite: a supportive coach, a selfless giver, a person who accepts others as they are without trying to change them. Wherever there's a dark shadow, there is a light at the other end casting it. Disowned virtues that you have believed could not be a part of you exist just below the surface, along with their counterparts. These you will see mirrored in persons you admire: heroes, movie characters, leaders, respected friends. By working through the conflicts with difficult people who enter your life, you come to observe the reflection of your "stuff." As you come to recognize your judgments of others as indications of aspects of your own rejected self projected onto others, you will realize that you are absent from other people's judgments of you. Your judgments are about you, and their judgments are about them.

What happens when you accept all parts of yourself? Do you act out your anger? Become a coward? This fear of opening a Pandora's box of our own worst qualities is what keeps many of us from owning all parts of ourselves. Your natural state is one of love for yourself and others. You do not stay in a state of fear and anger, greed or jealousy when you acknowledge those aspects of yourself. By turning around to look at them, and accepting their presence in yourself and others, you restore the natural state of peace.

Some people won't like it when you discover and share your authentic self. By "authentic," I mean that you accept all parts of yourself, even those that others do not. Perhaps you were quiet as a child and were told that you should be more sociable. When you went to your room alone to play, others thought you were withdrawn and sent you the message that something was wrong with you. Or maybe you were energized by talking to others, had many friends, and were very chatty—and you were told to "pipe down." Perhaps in your family, you received the message that tears were reserved for babies. Or perhaps you were an active person, always on the go, and the adults around you were quiet types. Maybe this difference led to a visit to the doctor's office to find out what medication you needed so that you could be more like them (and less like yourself). Perhaps you loved to create a world of fantasy, then later found yourself on a psychiatrist's couch, with your bewildered, no-nonsense parents fretting in the waiting room. Or perhaps your Ph.D. parents thought you threw away your life when you chose to pursue your dream to be an artist. If you have hidden or rejected a part of yourself—your wild enthusiasm, a tendency to be very active, your anger, your sadness, whatever it may be—then your uniqueness gets buried along with the disowned part. As we begin to let the real person appear through the persona we have created, some friends and acquaintances may be put off. Allow the people close to you the chance to get used to you as you really are. You will attract the people who accept you as you are. Others may fall by the way. Let them go. Accept their opinions for what they are: reflections of their own "stuff."

Forgiving Yourself and Others

In addition to the four elements identified by Dr. Susan Trout, a crucial fifth element completes the healing process: forgiving yourself and others. What happens to your body as you think and speak? Different emotions produce different chemicals in your body: Thoughts of love produce endorphins (which produce a positive effect on your body), and thoughts of fear produce adrenaline (which is helpful if you can use your nervous energy in physical activity, such as literally fleeing a dangerous situation, but it is harmful if you cannot). If you run from your fear because it makes you uncomfortable, the fear turns into anger or anxiety. Anger relates to past events; anxiety relates to the fear of what might happen in the future. Both emotions deny you the peace and love that exist in the present, and both create stress in your body.

The effect of stress on the body is extraordinary. In a psychology experiment, researchers placed rats in a container of water that offered no means of escape. They swam and swam until they were completely exhausted. Then the experimenters took them out of the water. Day after day, the rats were subjected to this daily stress. Autopsies on the animals later revealed that the rats' organs had aged at ten times their normal rate. Holding grudges causes stress like this on your body. This is why forgiveness is so vital. When you forgive someone of a supposed wrong to you, you are literally healing your own body. This point is illustrated further in the example that follows.

Joan Fountain, in describing her triumph of spirit, is particularly fond of using the expression "dancing on the bones of yesterday's sorrow."[8] Abused by both parents, she ate until she weighed 420 pounds. She built an armor of flesh to hide her pain and shame. Suicidal and fearful of the world outside her door, she didn't step outside for two years. Now, after having lost her excess weight, she is a successful motivational speaker, earning a six-figure income annually. At the center of her message is the importance of forgiveness in the healing process. She asks people to inquire about their own fear, look at it, and say, "You are a myth—you are behind me. I have lived through this. I will forgive those who perpetrated and forgive myself." She adds, "Then you weep for those who hurt you and for their pain, and you weep for the hurt that they experienced that caused them to hurt you. Only then have you gone through the forgiveness process. And at that point you can be free. You do not forgive people for them, you forgive them for yourself."

When you forgive and release someone, you release yourself. When we forgive ourselves, we are released—into health both physical and emotional. When we ask for forgiveness, we help the other person release himself of a grudge. What does this have to do with dealing with difficult people? Once you have gone through your past inventory of grudges (see Exercise 4 at the end of this chapter), you learn that you can release them as they come up. Because you lessen your "stuff" by forgiving and releasing those who harmed you, you are better equipped to handle the stressful events that you will inevitably encounter. In addition, when you are free of your resentments, you are motivated to forgive on the spot, as one man does in the story that follows.

> *Driving to work one morning, I observed the following interaction: Two cars ahead of me, a man driving an old, green Chevy appeared lost and was unable to decide whether to go straight or turn left. The man driving a new, black Oldsmobile immediately in front of me clearly wanted to turn left. His left blinker was flashing, he was honking his horn, and he shouted, "Move your car!" Although there was no mistaking his message, the driver of the Chevy continued his vacillation between going straight and turning left. I could see that he held a map at eye level, which he folded and unfolded in midair.*
>
> *I don't understand why he didn't pull out of the way to inspect the map along the side of the road, but his error in judgment did not justify the wrath of the*

Oldsmobile driver. Apparently satisfied that driving forward was the correct decision, the driver of the Chevy slowly drove through the intersection. I expected the Oldsmobile driver to turn left because he clearly had been eager to do so. However, he pursued the Chevy instead, deliberately colliding with the car's rear bumper.

The owner of the Chevy then pulled into a parking lot, not to inspect possible damage, but to read his map. The driver of the Oldsmobile pulled up beside him. The man in the Chevy, no longer oblivious, rolled down his window as the other driver got out of his car, slammed his door, and opened his mouth to speak. I expected the man in the Chevy to become similarly enraged because the other driver had rammed his bumper. Driving slowly through an intersection does not warrant a rear collision and a tirade of verbal abuse.

"I'm sorry I blocked your way," the man in the Chevy said agreeably. The other man's momentum was lost temporarily. After a pause, he shouted, "You should've pulled over! Now I'm late!" The first man did not point out the obvious, that the second driver had gone out of his way to antagonize him, greatly extending what initially was no more than a sixty-second delay.

"I'm sorry you're late," the first driver said with a look of real concern. "Well, I'm sorry, too," replied the other man, a double meaning in his softer delivery. He offered his card and said he would pay for any damage he had caused. His mood and behavior had changed dramatically and swiftly because of the forgiveness of the man in the Chevy.

The man in the Oldsmobile waved to the other man before driving off. The driver of the Chevy had brightened the day of three people: himself, the other driver, and me, the observer—all by taking care of business on the spot.

🐾 🐾

Each day, each moment, the condition of your bag of "stuff" determines whether you can extend love to others and to yourself. Instead of candy coating the bad feelings by denying past hurts, you can heal them. By going through the healing process, you come to understand that you are not confined to a life of a helpless victim. This understanding has the effect of allowing you to distribute love and kindness and to set boundaries without creating further conflict. It allows you to take a stand without alienating others. In this way of living, you can benefit from even unpleasant things that happen to you. To further assist you in your goal to release the "stuff" that interferes with your interaction with others, Chapter 6, "Satisfying the Inner Lion," addresses how to find meaning in your life, another key step in leaving your "stuff" behind.

🐾 🐾

Exercise 1: Reshaping Your Attitude

For one day, write down in your notebook each time you complain. Write down what you said and when you said it. Include silent complaints, that is, complaints you thought of but never spoke. Each evening or the next day, categorize your complaints. After the ones you can do nothing about, write the letter S (for "stuff"). After the ones you can do something about, write the letter A (for action).

Review the S list and identify the "stuff" that is bringing up these complaints. You might do this by writing in a journal or with expert help (see the list that appears after the exercises). Then review the A list and plan actions that you will take to make a difference. Write these on your calendar.

Finally, mark a day that you will—as an experiment—attempt to do no complaining. Instead, when you have a complaint on the tip of your tongue, sort your thoughts to find something encouraging to say. For example, instead of complaining about how busy you are, tell about something you are doing to create ease. Replace lamenting your lack of money with acknowledging that you're doing what you love. If you are deep in debt, speak of your plan to banish all credit spending and pay off debts. Cut past your complaints (you have rehearsed them enough) and get right to your solutions. With rare exceptions that you're unlikely to encounter in your daily life, there's always another, more positive aspect about a situation or person you can comment on.

Exercise 2: Accepting the Disowned Parts of Yourself

Go back to "Taking Stock," the exercise at the end of Chapter 3, in which you listed your judgments about the difficult people in your life and then crossed out the names in the first column and wrote "I" in their place. Take in as many of these disowned parts of yourself as you can. Imagine taking each one into your heart and accepting it as much as you can, even if the most you can do is love yourself for hating it. If you can't see how one applies, leave it for now. When you have accepted these traits in yourself as much as you can, picture the person you were originally judging, and do the same for him. Imagine yourself accepting him just as he is.

Exercise 3: Working with Your Shadows

Thank you to Robert Sellers, M.F.C.C., founder of Imaginal Therapy, who taught me the following process of using imagery to help people find the rejected parts of themselves and work out their inner conflicts.

Get a pencil, two pieces of paper or your notebook, and sit quietly where you will not be disturbed. Recall an interaction with a difficult person in which the situation brought up a stress response in you. Notice where the feeling is located in your body. Close your eyes and imagine a blank screen on which this feeling rises up, out of your body, and onto the screen, perhaps as an animal or a person. Watch it for a few moments to see what it does. Now draw a representation of this image.

Next, go through the same process to obtain a separate image for an animal or a person that represents the opposite feeling (that is, peace or love). Remember a time when you experienced this feeling, and notice where it is located in your body. Notice how it feels. Allow its presence in your body. When the feeling is strong, allow it to rise up, to become an image on your blank screen. When an image appears, watch it for a few moments to see what happens. Now write a story that contains the following: Both animals (or persons) go on a journey together and have to cross a river. They meet with three obstacles, one invisible (such as a power or person), one a natural force (such as a storm or fire), and the third an object that must be retrieved (such as a jewel). Have the first part of your story relate the meeting of these two opposites. Write about their relationship. Is it friendly? Antagonistic? The second part of the story will describe how they work together to get beyond the obstacles and retrieve the object.

In this last part of the exercise, by obtaining images for opposite parts of yourself, drawing them, and then writing about them, you move yourself along on your journey of integration of your disowned parts.

Exercise 4: Forgiving and Releasing Grudges

Take two sheets of paper or your notebook and consider all those persons, both dead and alive, for whom you hold grudges, and write down their names.

Part 1: Those Who Have Died

For the persons with whom you hold resentments who have died, write a letter each week, until you have included everyone on your list, expressing your hurt or angry feelings. Write about the situation in which you were hurt, how you felt about it, and how it damaged you. Say everything you want to express. Next, read your letter aloud, either to your reflection in the mirror, to another person you trust, or to an object you choose to represent the person.

Finally, burn the letter or tear it into tiny pieces as you recite the following: "I forgive you for any hurt I felt from what you did. I forgive you whether you intended to cause the hurt or you caused it unintentionally. I release you and let you go."

Part 2: Those Who Are Living

For those from your list who are living, determine which ones you are willing to communicate with directly. Place the letter C after their names. Next, write the letter W next to the names of those to whom you will write letters. For this group, note after each name whether you will mail the letter or destroy it. You will end up with three groups with whom you will communicate: those you will see face to face, those who will receive your letters, and those whose letters you will destroy rather than send. You will be the judge of which ones to send and which ones to destroy.

Rank the persons in the order in which you will take care of them, and write the dates on your calendar. For example, you might communicate with family members first, then friends. Cross the people's names off your list as you complete your communication of forgiveness with them.

I recommend beginning with asking each one for forgiveness. In the samples below, these requests are represented by A. The second part of your communication is represented by B, in which you will give examples of expressing your hurts and state your forgiveness. Anyone who might have resentments toward you will be released by your forgiveness. The one holding the grudge is the one hurt by it. Be sure to use language with which you are comfortable. Not everyone will use the language used below, especially in difficult situations. As you find your own phrasing, I strongly recommend that you speak from your own experience; that is, use "I" statements rather than "you" statements. Leave a pause after the first part of the communication to allow the other person a chance to respond. Often, the other person will make a spontaneous request for forgiveness, eliminating the need for the second part of your communication.

> A. *Younger sibling to older sibling:* "While we were growing up together, I must have been something of

a pain at times. I'm sorry for any times I caused you stress, and I ask your forgiveness. I love you. You are very important to me."

B. (After a pause) "When I couldn't find my allowance and saw it in your hand, I believed you had stolen it. I felt hurt and cheated and I yelled at you. If you did take it, I forgive you completely."

A. *Older sibling to younger sibling:* "When you were little, I was jealous of you. You didn't deserve my jealousy; you deserved my love. I'm sorry for any pain this caused you. Please forgive me. I love you."

B. (After a pause) "I hated it when you wore my favorite clothes without asking. I felt like you didn't care about me at all when you kept doing it even after I asked you to stop. I expected you to act like a grownup when you were a child. I forgive you for all the times you did this."

A. *Parent to child:* "When I raised you, I was often overwhelmed and impatient even though you deserved to be loved and cherished. I am sorry for those times, and I ask your forgiveness. You are so important to me, and I love you."

B. (After a pause) "I feel shut out by you when you don't accept that I won't buy you a car like your friend's parents did for him. It hurts me that you think it means I don't love you. I forgive you for not accepting me as I am."

A. *Child to parent:* "Sometimes, I wanted more from you than you could give. I took this personally instead of understanding that you, too, are human. I am sorry for not accepting you as you are. Please let me back into your heart."

B. (After a pause) "I hated it when you hit me and yelled at me [identify a specific time]. I felt like I was worthless. I forgive you for the times you did this. I release you and forgive you."

A. *To an ex-spouse:* "I'm sorry for blaming you for the failure of our marriage. I now know that my stress is my own and that you didn't cause it. I am especially sorry for [X]. Please forgive me."

B. (After a pause) "I was devastated when you did [X]. It made me feel [Y]. I forgive you completely for this and let you go."

❧ ❦

Other resources for expert help in healing your "stuff":

❧ Find a good therapist and set up counseling appointments.

❧ Locate the nearest Attitudinal Healing Center or Foundation for Inner Peace, and take a course.

❧ Buy a journal and make daily entries about your inner conflicts. Allow each side of the conflict full expression before you propose solutions.

❧ Take a course in shadow work.

❧ Read the book *Getting the Love You Want: A Guide for Couples*, by Dr. Harville Hendricks, or take one of his courses on how couples can heal one another with communication.

❧ Buy a copy of the book *Feeling Good: The New Mood Therapy*, by David D. Burns, M.D., and do the exercises in it.

6

SATISFYING THE INNER LION

We act as though comfort and luxury
were the chief requirements of life, when all
that we need to make us really happy is
something to be enthusiastic about.

—Charles Kingsley, quoted in *Walking on Alligators:*
A Book of Meditations for Writers

The wind, one brilliant day called to my soul
with an odor of jasmine.
"In return for the odor of my jasmine,
I'd like all the odor of your roses."
"I have no roses; all the flowers in my garden are dead."
"Well then, I'll take the withered petals and the yellow leaves
and the waters of the fountain."
The wind left. And I wept. And I said to myself:
"What have you done with the garden
that was entrusted to you?"

—Antonio Machado, Translated by Robert Bly "The Wind, One Brilliant Day"[1]

*T*he lion tamer sat on the grass at the animal entertainment park, brushing the sawdust from her jeans. Dandie, a three-month-old cub born in captivity to lions from the Serengeti Plain, crawled into her lap, nudging her hand for attention. She enjoys the public performances in the ring, but these private times, when she has an opportunity to bond with the animals, are her favorite. Lion tamers love animals and welcome the privilege of being able to be trusted by them and to learn their differing personalities and temperaments. Her profession offers her the satisfying combination of the physical and mental challenge of controlling the lions before a crowd and the thrilling reality that she is working alongside dangerous wild animals. She is not a large woman, and the smallest cat she works with in the ring is nearly eight feet long, weighs 350 pounds, and could strike down a fleeing 250-pound antelope with a single blow of its massive paw. It could overpower her in the brief time it takes for her to recognize her peril. Yet she cannot imagine another life for herself. Establishing a bond of trust and affection between herself and a wild animal offers her satisfaction that she could never begin to express, even to her closest friends. No one who observes her in this environment could ever doubt that she loves lions and that she loves the work she does.

This isn't true for all of us. Most of us lack the deep satisfaction that comes of linking our inner desires with the outward expression of our lives. The greater the gap between our inner and our outer lives, the more we generate the "stuff" that interferes in our interactions with other people. Do you feel an emptiness inside because you work in an unsatisfying job that doesn't allow you to use your talents? Staying in a job that you dislike creates chronic stress that accumulates and makes you irritable. If you work in your home or are retired, do you spend some of your day in activities that excite or please you? Does your life lack integrity? Your feeling of being in integrity directly reflects the trust that you have established with yourself. It's a deep feeling of ease that comes of knowing that wherever you go, you can trust yourself to act as you want to act and be the way you want to be. Like being in the company of a trusted best friend, being in integrity leaves you feeling safe with yourself, sheltered from harm. An environment such as this is inhospitable to fear. Being in integrity creates a sense of confidence and completeness, and it creates love for yourself and others. Finally, do you contribute to others with your time and money? If you leave no room in your day to help others and you keep all your money to yourself, you miss an opportunity to experience the good feelings that result from giving, and your "stuff" grows like weeds in a neglected garden.

If you ignore your inner needs in these areas, your unhappiness builds until it must find an outlet. Initially, it will turn inward on you and you will suffer alone, but eventually those around you will begin to suffer because of your unhappiness. The longer this situation continues, the less you are able to handle deadlines, crises, and difficult people. Fortunately, the reverse is also true: The more you increase your satisfaction in your life, the more you increase your ability to bring peace to yourself and those around you.

Like the previous two chapters, this one focuses on "stuff." Chapter 4 helped you to identify it in your own life. Chapter 5 recommended ways to heal it. This chapter also addresses the process of healing. Unlike Chapter 5, however, which focused on healing specific sources of "stuff" in your life—perhaps a broken romantic relationship or a childhood hurt—this chapter takes a larger view and encourages you to look inside yourself and examine the life you are living. Only such personal reflection can tame the lion within yourself. As this chapter discusses, satisfying your inner lion means keeping your soul fed by finding meaning in your everyday work, being in integrity, and making a contribution to others.

Finding Meaning in Our Everyday Work

Satisfying the inner lion requires bringing meaning to your working life. By "working life," I include not only what people do for employment, but also the financially uncompensated daily activities of those who tend to the household and those who are retired. Meaningful work brings a deep, pervasive feeling of satisfaction. It leaves little room for grumbling and complaining because you are too busy creating. Finding meaning in your work involves acknowledging and accepting things exactly as they are now and then taking steps to go on from there.

Frequently, you hear people making comments such as "I should have gone to college," or "I should have spent more time

with my children," or "I should have worked harder for that promotion." You may hear yourself making comparable statements
now and then. Dr. Wayne Dyer's mythical land of Eykis[2] includes a
rewind button that allows you, if you make a mistake or don't like
how something in your life turned out, to rewind the experience
and give it another try. In Eykis, it makes sense to say that you
should have done something differently because you literally have
the opportunity to try it again. I don't need to remind you that we
do not live in Eykis. Because no rewind button is available to us,
our life stands, exactly as it is at this moment. Accepting your life
as it is means leaving behind the tendency to wish you had done
things differently. If we wish to act differently in the present, we
certainly may, but feeling regret over how we acted in a past that
we cannot control is simply a waste of energy and a source of frustration. There is no room for the word should in our lives.

Much of the difficulty we face in finding meaning in our work
is that people push themselves too far to achieve "success" as it is
measured by others, success determined by what we possess:
objects of great beauty or expense, titles, degrees, money, and fame.
When we allow ourselves to be guided by the capricious, superfi-
cial demands imposed on us by others rather than heed the wise
voice within ourselves, we neglect our souls. And because what
happens to one of us affects us all, society as a whole suffers. We
encounter indications of this neglect every day.

A woman in her forties, a rising executive of a bank, participat-
ed in one of my classes and shared with us the story of her climb
to "success":

> I had been traveling the road of success in an external way:
> dressing for success, listening to be-all-you-can-be tapes, being
> trained in everything that was even remotely related to my
> field. "Success is enjoyable," I told myself, while filling in all
> my "empty" moments with more work. On a typical busy day,
> I was up at five, and by seven o'clock, I was at the office and
> ready to work. After a morning of meetings, I would eat lunch
> in my car in the fifteen minutes it took me to drive to the next

branch. Often, I needed to hastily remove food stains from my clothing before my next meeting. By evening, I felt exhausted from attending too many meetings, dealing with too many unsolved problems, and spending too many hours at the computer. By half past nine or so, I would drive home, dictating ideas for the next day's presentation into a hand-held tape recorder. Too many times, days would go by when I never even laid eyes on my children except when I looked in on them after they had already gone to sleep. The romantic relationship with my husband was a distant memory.

There were no gaps, no spaces in her life. She was a thing in motion. Because there was no time in her schedule that allowed her a moment of peace to step back and examine the life she was living, the choices she was making did not appear to bother her:

While at work, I could do it all because there was no time for thinking. The final straw came after I read an article about how you can give up some of your sleep time to have more hours in the day to work: The method involved getting you down to three or four hours per night by giving up sleep in half-hour increments, one week at a time. I decided to try it myself.

Dark circles gradually appeared under my eyes as I decreased my sleep time to make room for more work. I received concerned comments from co-workers about how much I was doing. My body became worn out, exhausted. Since I had no time to fix food, my mainstay became fast food from drive-through windows or food from the deli. I became increasingly irritable, and my team complained about me to my boss. My evaluation that year contained a single criticism: "Difficulty getting along with subordinates." There was little mention of all the extra hours I had put in, or the good work I had done, because my attitude was interfering with the well-being of others.

I wondered to myself, "What do I need to do to get back my top status?" Then, on a whim, I packed a picnic lunch, drove to the beach with Dutch, my Labrador retriever, and spent a badly needed day off. As the waves crashed and Dutch played happily, I began to have compelling thoughts: Suppose I were to keep rising within this company? What of it? Suppose I were to become CEO? What would I have to trade to maintain that position? What if I were really rich? Or famous? What would be different about this moment? I'd probably have a Winnebago or hotel suite and a cellular phone by my side.

Just then, Dutch nudged the palm of my hand with a stick she held in her mouth, and I became attentive to her in this precious moment. What is it about "work" that takes me away from being? How does that distracted experience—the one with an eye on the next goal—sneak up and gobble up my present moments?

What are you doing with the moments of your life? Donating them to activities you don't enjoy or don't find worthwhile? Are you doing what you love? Are you being who you are or who someone told you to be? Are you going at your own pace or someone else's? Most of us have the opportunity to inhabit a body for seventy years or more and the freedom to choose how we will spend that time. Many people know by the time they are thirty what budding talents they have, what they enjoy, and what they do not enjoy. Occasionally, we meet people who have fully embraced who they really are and not succumbed to cultural or familial pressure to be otherwise. These people are inspiring to us because they are guided by an inner voice; they are productive and happy, and their happiness is infectious. Wayne Dyer left a prestigious position as a college professor to write books in his robe. Oprah Winfrey rejected the sensational tone found on other daytime television shows and now strives to ensure that her show creates a positive influence and doesn't contribute to violence in the world. Mother Theresa spends her time with the ill and rejected, a gentle smile on her face.

There is a special purpose for you, and you are designed to play it out. But only you can discover what it is. You see that peace in the fisherman whose eyes shine as he speaks of his life on the sea, in the craft maker caressing her woodwork, in the tick-et taker at the theater who views each ticket as an opportunity to greet another person. Their eyes shine, alert and alive, and reflect deep satisfaction. These people have recognized their special pur-pose and now live their lives accordingly. Until you find your call-ing, the unhappiness in you mounts. To combat it, you erect a per-sona and go out into the world each day to do what you don't want to do. Then another person comes along with similar inner long-ings and pain, and both of you erupt, each thinking it is the other who is at fault.

Another woman living life in the fast lane made healthy adjust-ments in her life, then discovered an inner longing for expression of her neglected artistic self. This example shows that what each of us needs differs and can be determined only by us. While this woman needed a different line of work, someone else might need only to change the way he performs his current activities. At first, the woman thought that the distress she felt inside was the result of being too busy. She adjusted her schedule enough to be able to meet basic needs, such as eating healthy food, getting enough sleep, and spending time with her family, and for a while this change brought satisfaction. After two months with her life more in balance, her body felt better, but the gaps she had created pro-vided an avenue for her to notice the anxiety she felt about the kind of work she had been doing. As manager for the mobile home paneling division of Georgia Pacific, she delegated her artistic tal-ent to doodling while making business calls. Although her religion prohibited her use of tobacco and alcohol, much of her work required wining and dining prospective customers during the din-ner and evening hours.

The anxiety she felt was an ally. By paying attention to it, she was able to take the next step. She applied for and landed a posi-tion within the company that allowed her to do design work, using not only her creative talents, but also her managerial skills.

In this example, anxiety provided a clue to finding work more suitable to her talents. She took the time to examine the anxious feelings (her "stuff") that she had been running from for years. In her case, work provided a distraction from having to muster up the courage to attend to a deeper issue of being on a career track that was not right for her. Sometimes, this kind of distraction comes from a long-standing conflict with a person you have character-ized as difficult. People who get divorced thinking that their mate is the cause of their misery, for example, often are shocked to find themselves still unhappy after the divorce. If you are in such a long-standing conflict with yourself about your job or with a per-son, ask yourself: If this conflict magically cleared up, what would I be free to do? How much time do I spend ruminating and talking about this, and what is it I don't want to look at that is about me?

Researchers have made a discovery that provides an ugly but apt metaphor for what happens to us when we stay in jobs that we don't like. They discovered that although a frog placed into a pot of boiling water will immediately jump out, that same frog, when placed into a pot of cold water that is slowly being heated, will grow accustomed to the increasing heat and eventually will die in the boiling water.

When you choose one thing, you leave another behind. What are you choosing, and what are you leaving behind? Is there any-thing you are leaving behind that, if you discovered you were dying soon, you would regret leaving it undone? Do you have a special ability lying dormant? A creative project that you abandoned at the urging of someone else or your own inner critic? Are your kids raising themselves? Is your musical instrument or favorite sports equipment gathering dust? Is there anything you've been putting off dealing with? A dream goal? Forgiving long-standing grudges? These are the questions that can lead us to answers that will bring us fulfillment, a sense of being "on purpose."

Being "on purpose" means that you have matched your authentic self with your specific strengths and weaknesses, dis-covered work that requires your strongest skills, and are doing something that you are excited about. It's performing an activity that makes time "disappear." To paraphrase the Charles Kingsley quote that appears at the beginning of this chapter, all we need to be "on purpose" is an activity to be enthusiastic about.

Being in Integrity

To "be in integrity" is to be how you want to be in all settings. It involves keeping your word, being honest even during those times when no one else would know if you did something dishonest, speaking about people in their absence as you would if they were present, and being who you are rather than adopting a persona to please others. The truth about something is independent of what anyone thinks about it. The truth about you and your needs is likewise undeniable even if you've forced yourself into an ill-fitting mold.

When you are in integrity, you know peace. Because of the good relationship you develop with yourself when you are in integrity, a feeling of completeness accompanies you. You know that you can trust yourself in all situations to act in a way that you will be pleased with in retrospect. When you are in integrity and encounter a difficult person, your reaction is not harsh or critical. You might think to yourself, Oh, here's a person who must really be suffering. And then you would look for some way to make a connection with the person. I can remember when I felt like that, you might think, and I know how lost I was then. Perhaps you might wonder, How does someone get into that state? Or you might think, that could be me.

I think that the following story nicely illustrates the fundamental concept of being in integrity. A friend of mine first shared it with me twenty years ago. With each new year, the story means more to me.

> A king had two sons and gave each of them a chicken and a task: "Take this chicken to a place where no one else can see, and cut off its head. Whoever successfully accomplishes this mission will inherit my kingdom." The first son went deep into the woods, looked carefully around, and when he was certain no others were around, found a flat stump of a tree, where he cut off the chicken's head with one swing of his ax. He deposited the wriggling body into a burlap sack. Satisfied, he returned

to his father, imagining his riches. The second son returned
with the chicken intact, a worried expression on his face. "Oh,
Father," he said sadly. "I have failed. You see, everywhere I go,
the chicken sees." It was the second son who inherited his
father's kingdom.

To me, this tale promises rewards to those who live lives of
integrity. "Everywhere I go, the chicken sees," the son says to his
father. Clearly, he has empathy for the animal and cannot bring
himself to kill it even though his father has specifically instructed him to do so. Despite the promise of riches if he does otherwise, he stands by his beliefs. He maintains his integrity because
it is worth more to him, and because he is true to himself, he is
richly rewarded.

I believe that an objective integrity monitor accompanies us
and knows and sees all that we do. This is not a judging presence.
It is a part of each of us that is objective, that observes the whole
of our lives impartially. (Despite the nonjudgmental quality of this
monitor, sometimes, when we look back with regret at choices we
made and then take no steps to forgive ourselves and find ourselves making the same choices, we may feel an inner conflict that
becomes painful. This feeling may cause a belief in guilt that
causes separation.)

If I say something about someone that I would not say in the
person's presence, I lack integrity. If I say to someone, "I'll be
glad to do that," and then later complain to others that the person piled work on me, I lack integrity. By determining any areas
of your life where you are out of integrity and changing what
needs to change, you become peaceful within yourself and radi-
ate peace to others. The effect of being in integrity is similar to
the effect of forgiving someone. When you are out of integrity,
you are the one who suffers. By forgiving yourself for your past
and bringing yourself back in line with your integrity, you free
yourself from a belief that you are guilty. Exercise 5 at the end of
this chapter is provided to help you to identify and resolve areas
in your life where integrity is an issue.

Making a Contribution to Others

The healing effect of contributing to others is illustrated twice below. In the first example, an at-risk youth changes his life by spending time with senior citizens. The second is a look at how you might correct the effect of a bad day with a simple act of contribution.

Lonnie is a seventeen-year-old who attends a high school for students with emotional and behavioral difficulties. Debbie is fifteen-years-old. While she was away from the apartment buying formula, Lonnie watched their baby. The infant was crying and could not be consoled. The day before, Lonnie had been drinking heavily, and now, because of his throbbing head, each wail jangled his frayed nerves. He tried to soothe his son by changing his diaper, walking him around the room, and distracting him with a rattle. When the infant's cries grew more insistent, Lonnie shouted, "Shut up!" and struck the child. Then he fell on his bed, covering his ears to shut out the piercing sound. Debbie returned shortly afterward with the formula. She hurriedly prepared a bottle and fed the hungry infant.

Lonnie was so shaken by this incident that he accepted the help from the community that he had been refusing. He joined a group of others, like himself, who had been raised by one or more adults who suffered from alcoholism. Lonnie did not want to be like his stepfather, who had been similarly impatient with him as a child. Part of the help available to Lonnie was the opportunity to participate in a community service project arranged by his teacher and others to build self-esteem in at-risk students. He was assigned to spend time with elders who are separated from their families and mainstream community, much like Lonnie and the other youths who are placed in alternative schools.

Lonnie transports elderly citizens in wheelchairs from their rooms to physical therapy and serves them meals, feeding those who can't lift a spoon. Sometimes, he just talks with them. Lonnie is noticeably helped by these visits, and so are his elderly friends.

In an environment such as this, who is giving to whom? Both the kids and the elderly are giving to each other, and both groups benefit. These kids come from an environment in which stealing, abusing alcohol and drugs, attempting suicide, and killing are common. These actions are harmful, misguided attempts to relieve pain and obtain some inner peace. Drugs and alcohol temporarily bring the feeling of peace; beating up or killing someone, inmates report, makes them feel a momentary relief from their own misery; and suicide is perhaps the most desperate attempt to find peace. As those who participate in this program learn, the people who feel they are making a contribution to others through their daily activities are the only ones who are genuinely happy. They have discovered one of the true elixirs of life, a natural high that comes out of helping others.

For our second example, imagine that you are sitting at home in the evening recovering from the awful day you had. Outside, the rain is pouring, and you're hungry, tired, and lonely. In your refrigerator, you find a wilted carrot, an open can of tuna, and some fuzzy strawberries. Your mind scans the day you just had, landing on a humiliating incident with a difficult person that brought up anger. For several minutes, you think about that. You feel the stress increase in your body. You decide to write a scathing letter to the person. In your search for paper and pen, you come across a card you bought long ago for a friend. A smile crosses your lips when you see how perfect the card is for your friend, and you write a note inside it, expressing your affection and gratitude for the relationship. "You mean so much to me," you write, your handwriting flowing smoothly along with the good feelings you are creating inside yourself as fond memories of your friendship return to you. You address the envelope, apply a stamp, and bundle up to mail the letter. Once outside, you decide to pick up a delicious, hot sandwich for yourself. Back home, you hum to yourself as you heat up milk for a cup of hot chocolate. Feeling warm inside from your meal and your good deed, you recognize once more that giving and receiving are the same. What you gave to your friend you gave to yourself. This is the experience of contributing to others.

~✗ ✗~

The poet Antonio Machado asks, "What have you done with the garden that was entrusted to you?" As this chapter describes, one important way to tend to the garden within yourself and to heal your "stuff" is through doing meaningful work, being in integrity, and contributing to others. Those who do not tend to their own garden run the risk of becoming difficult themselves and having little tolerance for others who are being difficult. In Chapter 7, "Tools of the Trade," the focus shifts from you and the "stuff" that interferes with your interactions with others to those you find to be difficult. Now that you have learned how to heal the lion within yourself, you are ready to learn specific communication techniques that you can use in your personal interactions.

~✗ ✗~

Exercise 1: Accepting Yourself and Your Choices

This line represents your life line:

Birth_____Death

Age   0   10   20   30   40   50   60   70   80+

Put an X where you are on the line. Then sit in a comfortable position, become still inside, and visualize yourself being born. In your imagination, see yourself first as a baby, then as a one-year-old, a two-year-old, and so on, until you have reviewed the significant events from your past—from birth to the present moment—accepting it all as it is. Take ten to fifteen minutes to scan only the highlights (and low points). See yourself making all the choices you have made. Take it all into your heart and acknowledge that those experiences gave you the qualities that you have today. If there are areas that you cannot accept, write them down on a piece of paper under the heading: "I accept myself for hating these [choices/events]." Put those aside for a later time. At another time of your choosing, you might want to get extra help to work with this list (see the list of other resources that appears at the end of Chapter 5). Ask yourself the question "What would I need to accept this event?"

Exercise 2: Finding Your Qualities

In the exercise at the end of Chapter 3, you identified your disowned shadow parts. Taking these in and owning them as parts of yourself frees up the opposite, positive powerful parts of yourself that you have not recognized and owned. This exercise shows you that side of yourself.

List in your notebook the names of ten to twenty people you admire. Include celebrities, movie stars, friends, relatives, people you have read about in the newspaper. In a column beside the first one, list the qualities you like or admire about them. Next, look at that list of qualities. Are the qualities alike or different? Is there a pattern that appears? Does a theme emerge, such as creativity, dedication to service, playfulness at work, a no-nonsense work ethic? Does the job you now have allow expression of these attributes?

Now, cross out the names in the first column and write your name. The qualities that you have listed are qualities that you possess now. Do you recognize any of them in yourself today? Is there a change you could make in your current job to express any of these attributes? What do you find yourself doing in your free time? What activities make time "disappear" for you? What would be a next step toward manifesting those characteristics in your daily activities? Would it be doing something differently at your current job?

Next, on a piece of paper, write any possible changes that you could make to express some of these qualities in your daily activities.

Exercise 3: Considering a Shift in Career

The first step of this exercise is updating your résumé. When you have completed that step, go back to the list of qualities you created for Exercise 2. If these qualities existed in a single person, what occupations or activities would allow that individual to express them? Make a list of at least ten. Is there another kind of work that emerges as a possible option for you? Or is there a way to bring more of these qualities to your current life with a hobby or other activity?

Now, on a separate piece of paper or in a notebook, write down the names of other jobs that one person who possessed those qualities might have as his or her life's work. For this part of the exercise, you may want to make an appointment with a career counselor or conduct some research. See the "Further Reading" section in the back of the book for detailed bibliographic information on *Thank God, It's Monday* and *Do What You Love, the Money Will Follow*.

Exercise 4: Shaping Your Future

For some, this exercise will focus on employment; for others, it will relate to developing a talent or using a creative ability. Look again at your life line. How much room is left on the line? Is there anything you want to do that you haven't done yet? Look at the list of qualities you made for Exercise 2. Do you get a feeling of excitement thinking about any of them? Does one stand out to you? What do you find yourself thinking about as you look at these qualities? At this stage in your considerations, disregard the fears that may rise in you as you contemplate making changes for yourself. When you look at your life as a whole, what is it that you would regret not having done? Write down everything you can think of.

Exercise 5: Being in Integrity

Get into a comfortable sitting position and close your eyes. Review your life to date with the following question in mind: "Are there any incidents in which I was out of integrity that I need to do something about?" You may come up with incidents of regret. You may have harmed someone. You may owe money to someone else. You may feel that you are not giving enough to your job or, on the contrary, that you are giving too much to it, leaving your relationships out of balance. You may regret having lied to someone. You may have developed a habit of negatively characterizing others or of chronic complaining. On a separate sheet of paper or in a notebook, make a list of the incidents that come to mind.

Now, using this list, think of ways to bring yourself into integrity, and write them down. For example, you might write a letter of apology to the person you harmed, repay your debt, give more to your job, give more to the rest of your life, tell the truth, speak of others with love, or replace complaining with creativity. The act of simply preparing this list will begin to increase your trust in yourself, creating good feelings. When your list is complete, perform the activities that you have identified. If you list an activity that you cannot complete because it involves someone who is no longer a part of your life, perform a random anonymous (and related) act of kindness. For example, apologize to someone whom you choose to represent the person you really want to apologize to, give to the favorite charity of the person you had hoped to apologize to, or think of another option.

Exercise 6: Extending Love by Contribution

Select a percentage to represent a portion of your time or income each month (probably between 1 and 10 percent). Choose where this contribution of time or money will be directed each month. You might decide to contribute to the same group or individual each month, or you may select different benefactors. For example, one month you might donate $25 to a favorite charity. Another month, you might surprise someone who needs a lift with a gift, or you might present the person with a gift certificate for an hour or two of assistance that you will provide such as cleaning the person's home or updating her résumé. Or you might perform volunteer work for a nonprofit organization that helps people in your community, donate your time at a retirement home, spend time with a child who has no parents, gather a group of your friends to clean up a portion of the city, or plant a community garden. The opportunities to help others are endless and endlessly satisfying. Be creative and have fun.

7

TOOLS OF THE TRADE

Give us the tools and we will finish the job.
—Winston Churchill[1]

*T*he tools of her trade—a chair, a whip, a torch, lures—were close by. When the cat lunged, the lion tamer held out the chair, the wooden legs directed at the animal, and snapped the whip to protect her body. With a practiced signal, she vocalized and gestured a command confidently to the beast. The lion growled again, then whimpered, reluctantly dropping to the ground. She tossed a beef lure and he smacked it down, licking his lips and kneading the dirt in front of her with his claws. Then she scratched him behind the ears, and he purred.

Like a tamer of lions, you, too, will be rewarded with control in difficult situations when you use the appropriate tools. In earlier chapters of this book, I reviewed the importance of stretching your comfort zone, removing characterizations, and taking responsibility for and healing your "stuff." These skills form the foundation for the successful handling of all difficult situations. It is now time to discuss specific tools— that is, specific communication techniques—that have proven themselves useful in bridging the gap between difficult people and those willing to make the effort to reach them.

This chapter opens with a wonderful true story by Terry Dobson adapted from the pages of *Aikido and the New Warrior*, edited by Richard Strozzi Heckler. In this tale of conflict resolved on a train in Japan, we will see several basic lion taming skills at work:

- ❖ Listening without judgment
- ❖ Asking open-ended questions
- ❖ Using metaphors
- ❖ Spending time with the difficult person

After our look at these tools, I will discuss two others that are not shown in the story but that are important nevertheless:

- ❖ Building rapport (including mirroring posture, matching vocal volume, breathing in sync, and matching predicates)
- ❖ Using support-empathy-truth statements

In years of experimenting with responses to angry people, I have witnessed countless conflicts that at first appeared hopelessly deadlocked, but that moved forward as the one described in the following story did. After you read this story, I will discuss in detail each of the tools the older man uses so that you can then use them for yourself.

The train clanked and rattled through the suburbs of Tokyo on a drowsy spring afternoon. Our car was comparatively empty—a few housewives with their kids in tow, some old folks going shopping. I gazed absently at the drab houses and dusty hedgerows.

At one station the doors opened, and suddenly the afternoon quiet was shattered by a man bellowing violent, incomprehensible curses. The man staggered into our car. He wore laborer's clothing, and he was big, drunk, and dirty. Screaming, he swung at a woman holding a baby. The blow sent her spinning into the laps of an elderly couple. It was a miracle that the baby was unharmed.

Terrified, the couple jumped up and scrambled toward the other end of the car. The laborer aimed a kick at the retreating back of the old woman but missed as she scuttled to safety. This so enraged the drunk that he grabbed the metal pole in the center of the car and tried to wrench it out of its stanchion. I could see that one of his hands was cut and bleeding. The train lurched ahead, the passengers frozen with fear. I stood up.

I was young then, some twenty years ago, and in pretty good shape. I'd been putting in a solid eight hours of Aikido training nearly every day for the past three years. I liked to throw and grapple. I thought I was tough. The trouble was, my martial skill was untested in actual combat. As students of Aikido, we were not allowed to fight.

"Aikido," my teacher had said again and again, "is the art of reconciliation. Whoever has the mind to fight has broken his connection with the universe. If you try to dominate people, you are already defeated. We study how to resolve conflict, not how to start it."

I listened to his words. I tried hard. I even went so far as to cross the street to avoid the chimpira, the pinball punks who lounged around the train stations. My forbearance exalted me. I felt both tough and holy. In my heart, however, I wanted an absolutely legitimate opportunity whereby I might save the innocent by destroying the guilty.

"This is it!" I said to myself as I got to my feet. "People are in danger. If I don't do something fast, somebody will probably get hurt."

Seeing me stand up, the drunk recognized a chance to focus his rage. "Aha!" he roared. "A foreigner! You need a lesson in Japanese manners!"

I held on lightly to the commuter strap overhead and gave him a slow look of disgust and dismissal. I planned to take this turkey apart, but he had to make the first move. I wanted him mad, so I pursed my lips and blew him an insolent kiss.

"All right!" he hollered. "You're gonna get a lesson." He gathered himself for a rush at me.

A fraction of a second before he could move, someone shouted "Hey!" It was earsplitting. I remember the strangely joyous, lilting quality of it—as though you and a friend had been searching diligently for something, and he had suddenly stumbled upon it. "Hey!"

I wheeled to my left; the drunk spun to his right. We both stared down at a little, old Japanese man. He must have been well into his seventies, this tiny gentleman, sitting there immaculate in his kimono. He took no notice of me, but beamed delightedly at the laborer, as though he had a most important, most welcome secret to share.

"C'mere," the old man said in an easy vernacular, beckoning to the drunk. "C'mere and talk with me." He waved his hand lightly.

The big man followed, as if on a string. He planted his feet belligerently in front of the old gentleman, and roared above the clacking wheels, "Why the hell should I talk to you?" The drunk now had his back to me. If his elbow moved so much as a millimeter, I'd drop him in his socks.

The old man continued to beam at the laborer. "What'cha been drinkin'?" he asked, his eyes sparkling with interest. "I been drinkin' sake," the laborer bellowed back, "and it's none of your business!" Flecks of spittle spattered the old man.

"Oh, that's wonderful," the old man said, "absolutely wonderful! You see, I love sake too. Every night, me and my wife (she's seventy-six, you know), we warm up a little bottle of sake and take it out into the garden, and we sit on an old wooden bench. We watch the sun go down, and we look to see how our persimmon tree is doing. My great-grandfather planted that tree, and we worry about whether it will recover from those ice storms we had last winter. Our tree has done better than I expected, though, especially when you consider the poor quality of the soil. It is gratifying to watch when we take our sake and go out to enjoy the evening—even when it rains!" He looked up at the laborer, eyes twinkling.

As he struggled to follow the old man's conversation, the drunk's face began to soften. His fists slowly unclenched. "Yeah," he said. "I love persimmons, too. . . ." His voice trailed off.

"Yes," said the old man, smiling, "and I'm sure you have a wonderful wife."

"No," replied the laborer. "My wife died." Very gently, swaying with the motion of the train, the big man began to sob. "I don't got no wife, I don't got no home, I don't got no job. I'm so ashamed of myself." Tears rolled down his cheeks; a spasm of despair rippled through his body.

Now it was my turn. Standing there in my well-scrubbed youthful innocence, my make-this-world-safe-for-democracy righteousness, I suddenly felt dirtier than he was.

Then the train arrived at my stop. As the doors opened, I heard the old man cluck sympathetically. "My, my," he said, "that is a difficult predicament, indeed. Sit down here and tell me about it."

I turned my head for one last look. The laborer was sprawled on the seat, his head in the old man's lap. The old man was softly stroking the filthy, matted hair.

As the train pulled away, I sat down on a bench. What I had wanted to do with muscle had been accomplished with kind words. I had just seen Aikido tried in combat, and the essence of it was love. I would have to practice the art with an entirely different spirit. It would be a long time before I could speak about the resolution of conflict.[2]

Using powerful tools of communication, instead of a whip and chair for protection, the hero in the story interacts with the difficult person without characterizing him. He does not add to the conflict by projecting his "stuff." Instead, he listens without judgment, asks open-ended questions, uses metaphors, and spends time with the other man. These are tools you no doubt already use with "easy" people, such as your friends. By becoming more conscious of them, you can transfer your use of these tools to difficult situations.

Listen without Judgment

Nonjudgmental listening involves being comfortable as others speak their difficulties without trying to change them. It involves allowing people to find their own answers. In the story, the old man listens to the drunken man's verbal assault on the riders in the train and then invites him to sit down and talk about it. Allowing someone full expression, without trying to move the person along to a more acceptable emotional state and without succumbing to the desire to give advice, allows him to discover the source of his anger, vent his feelings, and then come up with his own answers.

Just for today, find an opportunity to be with someone who is angry, and don't try to change the person's mind or talk the person out of his anger. Just be in the presence of it, and listen nonjudgmentally for understanding. Keep your opinions to yourself unless someone asks you for them.

Ask Open-ended Questions

Of course, during your encounters with difficult people, you will not always be silent. When you speak, remember to ask open-ended questions, which, like your listening, will not involve judgment. Be careful to ask questions that contain no bias in tone or phrasing. Your concern here is to get the person to speak about what troubles him, not to provide guidance or to criticize. In the tale, we see the older man inquire about what the other man has been drinking. Even though the man responds angrily, the man in the kimono continues to appeal to the man with respect and without judgment. Reading the story, one can sense that the old man sees the laborer as more than his anger.

Examples of open-ended questions include the following:

* What bothers you most about this?
* What does that feel like to you?

* What have you considered about this?
* How does this differ from what you were expecting?
* What will be your next step?
* What would it be like if that happened?
* What was your role in all of this?
* What does that mean to you?
* What is the sadness about?
* Will you put your anger [sadness, frustration, and so forth] into words?

In addition, you might ask for clarification if something said by the other person is not clear to you. Again, be careful to keep all bias out of your questions. Here are a few examples:

* Do you mean that you felt put down by what I said?
* When did you begin to feel this way?
* What do you think the other person intended?
* Are you saying that you have given up on this relationship?
* What did that mean to you when your suggestion was ignored?
* What is the worst thing about this for you?

Most of us consider ourselves to be good listeners, but listening well while under stress is a skill that requires practice. I know you think that you listen well, but do you remember to listen to someone who is angry or frustrated? I don't mean look as if you're listening, then jump in at the first opening to offer your own viewpoint; I mean getting into the other person's shoes and being in the presence of the anger without allowing your response to be affected by your "stuff." Usually, people defend their position, fight back, or freeze in fear. It requires real effort to keep yourself from giving advice. So does developing patience while people find their own answers. Empathy necessitates putting judgment aside so you can create a safe, nonpunitive environment.

Use Metaphors

The use of metaphor with difficult people is powerful because metaphors bypass fear and the intellect and go directly to the gut or subconscious. Some would argue that using metaphors deliberately in difficult situations is sneaky and manipulative. I look at it as an effective way to extend love and shorten the time needed to resolve conflict. Strictly speaking, a metaphor is a figure of speech in which a word or phrase that literally means one thing is used in place of another to suggest a likeness between them. I use the term more broadly to mean the use of language to conjure images in the mind of the listener.

In the story, the old man talks about his wife and his persimmon tree while imbedding a message that validated the drunken man: "I'm sure you have a wonderful wife." The images he creates with his words shift the focus in the attacker's mind from hostility in the train to the tree and happier times. This shift helps to reveal the source of the man's anger: grief. It also helps put the laborer at ease because he now knows something about this stranger in the kimono who had the courage to interact with him even in the face of his threatening behavior. In addition, when the older man states that his tree weathered an ice storm better than he expected, he provides hope to the man that he will emerge from the storminess of his own life, and when the talk turns to enjoying the evening even when it rains, the older man's language suggests the possibility that the drunken man will be released from his pain through the shedding of his tears.

Stories create images and lead the difficult person to make pictures in his own mind. A metaphor can switch a person from imagining his own frustration and anger to imagining whatever picture you paint with your words. How do you know which metaphor to use? For most of us, the choice comes instinctually. Suppose you went to Hawaii and had a wonderful time. Later, a friend says, frowning, "I might go to Hawaii, but I don't know. . . . It's so expensive." You respond, "Oh, yes! We had to scrape to save enough for a trip to Maui, but was it ever worth it! Wow! The warm oceans, fresh fruit and fish, carefree spirit. I loved the snorkeling. Those fish came right up to us and ate food right out of our hands! I ate coconut-macadamia nut pancakes that were delicious!" The language goes beyond mere description. It captures a mood by painting a picture so vivid that it invites your listener into the scene. Because how we feel is determined by what we say to ourselves and picture in our minds, the listener is going to be positively affected by what he imagines.

Spend Time with the Difficult Person

You are much more likely to handle a difficult person effectively if you are willing to spend time with him and get to know him (and yourself). This means that you take the time to remove any characterizations of the person as difficult, work on your "stuff," examine your judgments of the person to see how they mirror what needs to be healed in you, and imagine the situation turning out ideally. Many of us, after hearing such a list, would respond, "But I don't have the time for that." But when you consider both the time you waste and the energy you expend reacting to the difficult situation and the knowledge that the situation will not improve on its own (so you can look forward to the same conflict in the future), then the better alternative becomes clear. Use your time proactively to build something positive that will last. I think you'll find that in the long run you not only have a better result, but you've spent less time and energy to achieve it than you would have spent allowing the conflict to remain.

More Lion Taming Skills

In addition to the skills illustrated in the story above, the following text relates two others that can be helpful when dealing with difficult people: building rapport and using support-empathy-truth statements.

Build Rapport

Knowing how to build rapport with a difficult person is a helpful skill, especially when situations are volatile, and the skill isn't difficult to learn. In fact, to some extent, you use this skill automatically when you speak with a friend. When I refer to the skill of building rapport, I am referring to four specific skills: mirroring posture, matching vocal volume, breathing in sync, and matching predicates. Notice for yourself that when you are talking to someone you easily get along with, your posture roughly mirrors that of your partner, your vocal volume is approximately the same as the other person's, the two of you are breathing in sync, and you even match predicates frequently. Just as you do with your friends, you can use all these skills at once in difficult situations, but I recommend practicing them one at a time until they come easily to you.

Mirror Posture. The older man in the story did not mirror the laborer's posture. If he had wanted to do so, he would have stood (slowly, so as not to appear challenging) so that he could be face to face with the other man and make level eye contact with him. In this situation, however, it was wiser to stay seated. He needed to get the man's attention immediately to avoid the impending fight, and effectively mirroring posture with the man would have required more time than he felt was available to him. Generally, though, I recommend roughly mirroring the other person's posture in difficult situations because you will make a link with the other person even though he won't be aware of it. It is one more step toward mending the severed connection between the two of you. If you've ever been in a conversation in which the other person sits in a laid-back position when you are feeling tense, or he turns away frequently while you are speaking, you know what it feels like to be separated from someone even in the midst of a conversation. By mirroring posture with the difficult person and making eye contact, you make it clear that you care enough to participate with the other person completely. If he is standing, stand. If he is sitting, sit. If he is leaning forward, do the same. Whether you are standing or sitting, try to use some of the same physical gestures as the other person when you speak with him, but be careful not to create the impression that you are mimicking his behavior, which could aggravate the situation.

Match Vocal Volume. When someone is so angry that he is shouting at you, especially if he is shouting to gain power (see the discussion on the hostile lion below), raise your vocal volume until it is slightly below his. If the person is prone to outbursts, however, this may not be the best technique because it could make the other person even more angry. Regardless of the vocal volume you select, keep the content of what you say benign, friendly, or even loving. Some examples include the following:

- ✤ "Yes, I can see how important this is to you!"
- ✤ "Of course!"
- ✤ "I can see you want this very badly."
- ✤ "Yes! Tell me more about this."

Similarly, if the person you are speaking with is soft-spoken and you tend to speak exuberantly and rapidly, slow your pace and lower your volume, and you will have an easier time establishing rapport.

Breathe in Sync. I once went to a party filled with engineers I had never met. At the time, I was learning about synchronized breathing and its role in building rapport. To amuse myself at that otherwise boring party, I did nothing but pace and match breathing (is it rapid and shallow or deep and slow?). It's not easy! You have to watch someone's shoulders going up and down or stomach going in and out and pace your own breathing to his, either slowing yours down or speeding it up. The tricky part of this technique is to be able to pull it off without being noticed and thought of as strange. If the shoulders are not moving enough for you to see, you have to watch the stomach move in and out. It can be difficult, but if you are successful, you will establish the rapport you seek, and the other person won't even be aware of why the situation has improved. I had been to parties like that party of engineers before, but I'd never seen anything like what I saw that night. Call it coincidence, but by the end of the evening, I was literally surrounded by people wanting to talk to me! People were coming up to me and starting conversations, sitting next to me on the couch, acting as if we had known each other for years. Try it at a party or meeting and see for yourself.

Match Predicates. Matching predicates, another component of rapport building, can help someone to feel understood and so reduce conflict. By predicate, I mean any word that helps to express what is said about the subject of a sentence—typically a verb, although I also include adjectives, adverbs, and even nouns. The reason this technique establishes rapport is that each of us tends to think and speak predominantly in visual, auditory, or kinesthetic terms, and when we encounter a person with the same preference, we feel that we have discovered a kindred soul. Thus, in your conversations with difficult people, try to use language in a way that reflects their preference so that they will feel that you truly understand what they are saying.

Let me give you a few examples. If you match his "Get out of my face" with a sentence with a kinesthetic predicate, such as "I guess you don't feel like being with me right now," you will establish rapport. If you respond with a statement without a kinesthetic predicate, for example, "You don't see us together right now" (visual), or "I hear you saying you don't want to talk now" (auditory), rapport isn't likely to occur. If you respond to "I told you to do the dishes. Don't you ever listen to me?" (auditory) with "Hey, I'll handle it" (kinesthetic), the other person probably will not feel understood. But if you respond with "When you say something, you want me to hear it" (auditory), you help to enhance communication because you are speaking in the individual's preferred predicate system. The following are three brief lists of frequently used predicates, shown by predicate system:

Visual

see	reveal
look	picture
outlook	clarify

view	bright
image	examine
imagine	viewpoint
clear	show
dream	vision
appear	seem
paint	vivid

Auditory

remark	announce
tell	buzz
say	mention
discuss	hear
listen	grumble
inquire	communicate
tone	argue
speak	inform
disclose	dispute
question	roar

Kinesthetic

grasp	smooth
tough	soft
damage	hanging
injure	hit
concrete	stir
hard	grab
feel	warm
handle	cool
dangling	seize
stress	grope

Matching predicates often happens automatically when people are in rapport, but deliberately using this technique takes practice.

For practice, listen for predicates in a variety of environments. Listen to songs on the radio and decide which predicate system predominates. Watch talk shows or other television programs and listen for predicate preferences. Once a day, call a relative or friend and ask her what she has been up to and listen for predicates. Talk with the grocery clerk and do the same. You spend your day surrounded by them, but unless you listen closely, you won't notice them.

Use Support-Empathy-Truth Statements

The support-empathy-truth (S.E.T.)[3] statement is successful even with people who do not have the ability to imagine another's viewpoint. It is used when you want to set a boundary with someone who is so engrossed with himself that he is unable to imagine future consequences. The support portion invokes a personal statement of concern. The empathy segment attempts to acknowledge the person's chaotic feelings. The truth statement, or "I" statement, is your own personal truth. Do not use the word "but" to join separate parts of your S.E.T. statements because doing so tends to cancel out what comes before. Instead, use pauses or the word "and". Here are a few examples:

* (To someone yelling angrily at you) "This is important. I care about this. I can see how frustrated you are about it and I want to deal with this. (Pause) Not this way." (And then you suggest a later time when you might solve the problem together.)
* (To a child) "I'm sorry you're feeling so bad. It must be frustrating to have a little brother ruin your things. I can't let you hurt him."
* (To a suicidal person) "I care about how bad you are feeling, how painful this must be for you. I cannot allow you to hurt yourself."

The combination of support and empathy with truth included in the S.E.T. statement, allows the difficult person to know you understand and empathize with him. It validates the person but also sets necessary limits on the person's behavior. It also allows you to feel good about how you handled the situation no matter what the outcome, because it allows you to express your concern and to state your truth. Often, one or the other or both go undisclosed in interactions with difficult people, leaving only the boundary, or "no," statement.

Hostile Blamers and How to Deal with Them

You already have improved your relationships. Have you noticed? Sometimes, things go so smoothly that you don't even recognize the change in yourself. Your comfort zone is larger, you are regularly removing characterizations, and you are healing your own "stuff." You are no longer contributing to the fear. Instead, you are increasing well-being in the world. You are a force for peace.

If you would like additional guidance on how to deal with those lions who use anger to move people to get what they want—those who criticize and blame others rather than take responsibility and those who generally are pleasant but who sometimes explode from stored up "stuff"—then read on. I've gathered a few examples from my own experience to show you how some of these skills can be used in actual moments of conflict.

The Hostile Lion

Why does the hostile lion act as he does? Because he has learned that people move out of his way when he spews his anger. What power! What sway! Mostly, he enjoys the conflict and feelings of omnipotence. He views the world as chaotic, and he recognizes his anger as a means to gain some element of control. So where's the fear I keep speaking of? The hostile lion rarely shows the fear behind his anger and in some cases is not aware of it himself. He is a wizard at turning his fear into anger as soon as it appears. Sometimes, you catch a glimpse of it on his face before it is transformed into anger. During times of stress at home and in the office, the hostile lion feels such a loss of control that he fears impending disaster. It feels better, for a while, to hurt someone else. For a moment, he gains control over something—that is, you.

Some hostile lions want to be kind but leave so many truths undelivered that eventually they erupt with pent-up anger in response to a minor incident. Listening is one way to help these lions return to their more natural state. In cases where you have your own "stuff" interfering, get a break in the interaction if you can or listen actively, until the buildup is completely vented.

When dealing with the hostile, aggressive lion, people often can be counted on to placate, submit, and feed the fear side or to respond in kind with hostility, delivering their truth but in a way that scorches, escalating the conflict. The following example shows the most effective technique for dealing with the person who uses anger to get his way; standing up to him without adding to the conflict. This is done by meeting his vocal volume but keeping the content of your words benign or even loving, and by naming what is happening, or delivering your truth. Stand up to these invalidators you must, or they will not respect you and they will increase their bullying behavior.

A Hostile Blamer

I attended a meeting with Mr. Wilson and several others, including his wife, a program manager, a child advocate, and two teachers, to plan a schedule for his son. He was wearing a Rolex watch, pin-striped gray suit, and red silk tie. When his portable telephone began to ring, he set his briefcase on the conference table, opened it, and answered the phone inside. "Edna, I told you to hold all calls," he said to his secretary. "How do you expect me to get anything done?"

During the meeting, his wife sat demurely beside him, twisting and pulling at the handkerchief in her lap as if it might give her strength. While he blamed the school district for their son's problems, she simply nodded her head.

One of the committee members mentioned that the boy had thrown a typewriter at his teacher and was suspended from school for the seventh time. "Of course!" Mr. Wilson bellowed. "That was during reading. Back in third grade, they never taught him how to read." His loud, accusatory tone suggested that the present company was somehow to blame.

Somewhat to my surprise, my physiology registered an excited sensation, a far cry from the queasy feeling I had grown accustomed to in situations like this one. I recognized an opportunity to try out what I know with a difficult person. I noticed the others at the table increasing their politeness and deference to the man, a placating behavior I recognized immediately, having repeated it so many times myself. With some, the kindness tactic works—not, however, with a man such as this, who enjoys seeing people move out of the path of his aggression.

"What would you like to see happen?" one woman at the table carefully asked the man. His wife started to comment when he interrupted. "You haven't helped by babying him," he said to his wife. "He's a lazy bum!" Then, turning to the teacher, he said, "I expect you to teach him how to read and behave and have respect." He paused. "Whatever happened to kids respecting their elders?" he demanded rudely, as if we were directly responsible for his son's manners. "This is your problem, not mine."

In similar interactions, it is at this point that someone will attempt to shift the blame, for example, "If you can't control him at home, how do you expect his teacher to be able to control his outbursts in a classroom of thirty-seven?" Or perhaps someone will offer a counterdig: "You are the parents. It's your fault your son is so screwed up."

This is not the time for arguing. This is the time to check silently for characterizations, to check to see if your "stuff" is affecting your behavior, and then to figure out what you will say or do after you've considered these two factors. Without doing that, your efforts will not be fully effective, and you might even add to the conflict.

I didn't know yet how I would respond, but I felt a sureness, a comfort level, a burst of energy similar to that when the police officer pulled me over and I pretended to be ordering from a drive-up window. I thought silently to myself, "This team is bigger than whatever it's stuck in right now. Mr. Wilson is bigger than his anger. His wife is bigger than her fear and judgment. Each one in this room has unlimited potential." I quieted my mind and listened for a signal from my Intuitive Knower. There was no message, only stillness. Then an odd thought occurred to me. It was a concept from dog training called gaining alpha with your dog. Dogs are pack animals and will naturally attempt to gain alpha, or become top dog, over the pack. It is in the dog's best interest if the dog owner remains in the alpha position in case of danger—for example, if the dog runs into the street. A person obtains alpha by using a loud tone of voice and taking charge. "This man is gaining alpha," I realized. "He's telling us all to sit and beg."

I presented my report on their son, which stated that the boy was not emotionally disturbed, but was instead demonstrating "conduct problems." I briefly detected a look of relief, then sadness, in the man's face, attributable, I learned much later, to his buried grief over the chaotic state of his relationship with his son. Within a few seconds, however, he was back on track. "Well, what are you people going to do now?" he demanded angrily. "What use is any of that to me? I've got an attorney, and we'll see whose problem this is."

I was under attack. He was looking right at me, leaning forward, his arm on the table, pointing his finger for emphasis. I felt the fight or flight response battling within, so I took a breath, acknowledged the presence of my "stuff" and set it aside, and elevated the volume of my voice so that it was just under Mr. Wilson's.

"I've been hearing a lot of invalidating," I said matter-of-factly, "You've blamed the third grade teacher, these teachers, your son, your wife. I don't see how we can work as a team when you keep intimidating people." His eyes were riveted on me, challenging. I continued, lowering to my natural volume. "We could go on arguing like this all day. I have opinions that I could spend hours venting, but we would still disagree about what needs to happen. I am not willing to spend the time arguing and blaming. If we can work as a team, honoring our differences, and figure out a solution, then I am willing to continue. If not, we might as well adjourn now and appeal to higher powers, as you have suggested."

Mr. Wilson did a double take, as though noticing there was a person sitting in my chair for the first time. After that, the tone of the meeting shifted, and we were able to find a solution. After the meeting, he sought me out to suggest lunch. Such a shift in attitude is not uncommon in situations like this. Bullies respect those who stand up to them without adding to the conflict.

A Hostile Blamer on the Telephone

I was talking on the telephone when my secretary came into my office to show me a message she had just taken. A light on my phone flickered on and off, signifying a caller on hold. Sarah Jane, a parent of a student at one of my schools, was demanding to talk with me. The length and content of the message, together with the look on my secretary's face, told the story: I would be dealing with a difficult person. That knowledge is helpful. It brings an objectivity that allows you to avoid taking things personally.

I ended my telephone conversation. Then I closed my eyes for a moment and imagined that I was surrounded by a protective white light. I recalled a favorite quote from Longfellow: "If we could read the secret history of our enemies, we should find in each man's life sorrow and suffering enough to disarm all hostility." Then I took a deep breath and took the other call. "Hello, this is Betty Perkins," I began. Without pause, Sarah Jane spat rather than spoke, "Where have you been? I never see you out there! You're supposed to be there on Mondays!" In my mind, I saw her as huge, forbidding. For a moment, I wanted to recount to her my busy week, to tell her how many programs I serve, perhaps folding in how underappreciated I am. Discarding that notion, I considered sarcasm: "Wait a minute, I only let my mother talk to me like that." But she was not calling to find out about my schedule, and she was not seeking sarcasm. She was in pain and seeking relief.

"So you're frustrated from trying to reach me?" I responded at a volume and verbal pace much like hers. "Yeah! You're never there," she repeated. "And I talked to someone here who says you're only here one hour a week."

She thought I should be at that school all day, all week. She didn't know how I cover my programs, flying by the seat of my pants, and she didn't care. What she wanted was to get some control, some energy, a handle on her fear. I felt that I was starting to lose control, so I put her on hold. Sometimes, you have to resist the urge to defend yourself during an attack unless you want to add fuel to the already raging fire. This instance was difficult for me because she struck a raw nerve of mine: having too much to do and not being able to complete everything or please everyone.

In a few moments, after I had regained my center and refueled my energy, I returned to the call: "Hello, again. Thank you for waiting. Now where were we? Oh, yes, you were saying that I'm at your daughter's school only one hour a week. Actually, I think that's a rather generous estimate." There was a distinct pause from her end of the line. The brief break and my comment had slowed her building momentum. When you agree with an attacker's comment, the stress is dissolved. She took another approach. Because I was not feeding the anger-blame-guilt loop by succumbing to feelings of guilt, she aimed her blame at another target, her child's teacher. After a long story in which she accused one of her daughter's teachers of meanness, we arranged a meeting.

When we met, I was surprised at how small she actually was. The meeting was easier for me than the telephone call. I can remove my characterizations easily in someone's presence. I remembered that we are equal beings and that she is bigger than whatever she is temporarily stuck in. Listening to her story, I removed my characterizations one by one. There was only one dicey moment: She described a gun waiting in her glove compartment. "I don't take nothin' from no one," she declared, presumably to make certain that I took her seriously. My peace was sent reeling with images of being shot down as I carried my briefcase to my car at the end of my day. With a little extra effort, I once more removed my characterization of her as a difficult person. At the end of the meeting, she hugged me hard, smiling.

A Hostile Lion in the Office

I was practicing with a difficult woman, doing research on rapport-building skills. This is a woman whom most people either avoid or tiptoe around. I had achieved a measure of acceptance with my obsequious placating behavior, but I wanted to venture something a little more bold and honest. Although she did not hold a prominent position, she held power over anyone who called or came within five feet of her. On this day, I needed to ask her for something from one of her files, and I could tell by her expression that it wasn't a good day. Had I not needed the information, I gladly would have forgotten the whole thing.

After I asked for the file, she stood up, slammed things down, and went about extracting it from her cabinet in a frustrated and exasperated manner. I decided to mirror her gestures and wondered what the effect would be. I matched her actions by slamming down the file I was holding. Her extreme annoyance became a rage. Papers flew, and her expletives drew a crowd. In situations like this one, I recommend taking this kind of reaction not as a sign of failure but as feedback. I saw how vulnerable she was, not how powerful, as her anger might have led some people to believe.

An irony of the bully is that even though he gives out abuse daily, he is hypersensitive to criticism and anger himself. In this example, even though the woman was rude and verbally abusive to most of the people who came into contact with her, she felt justified in her behavior, viewing it as standing up for herself while she was under some kind of perceived attack. When others used the slightest pressure on her, or when a parent arrived at the school under stress or pressed for time, this woman would boil into a rage as if she were being picked on. Her anger, so close to the surface, could be tapped with a glance. If a parent needed to pick up a child for a doctor's appointment, and the other office worker was away on a break, heaven help the unsuspecting mother or father who approached this woman with a request.

In an effort to improve my relationship with the woman, I decided to alter my approach in obtaining information from her. The next time I needed to ask her for something, I called ahead, letting her know when I would be arriving and what I needed. She was not bothered by the call or my request. I asked her if it worked better for her when I called ahead. Obviously pleased that I was considering her needs, she said, "Oh, sure. Let me know what you need, and I'll get it." When I arrived, I greeted her by name and smiled. Each time I saw her, no matter what her mood, I separated my "stuff" and spoke to her as if she were warm and loving. I told her about my kids and asked about hers. I became one of the few people she looked forward to seeing.

A Young Hostile Blamer

In this example, we look at a hostile blamer who is still young. The fear in him is carefully covered over by his anger, but it is a little more accessible than it tends to be in the adults I meet. I used to work at a continuation high school with kids in a class for the "seriously emotionally disturbed." Some of them were actually "conduct disordered," meaning that they didn't go by the rules, they became violent, and some of them committed crimes. Sometimes, they were placed in that class because no one else wanted to deal with them. Johnny was one such student. His brief stay in a regular high school ended when he was kicked out for insubordination, selling drugs on campus, and constantly intimidating and belittling the other students. His psychological reports and school records stated that Johnny had an "antisocial personality disorder" and lacked remorse. They went on to say that he hurt others for his own pleasure. To remove my characterization of him as a kid with no redeeming qualities, I imagined him as a baby, being held and cuddled by his mother.

When I sent for Johnny and he responded with belligerence, I remembered the image of him as a precious child. I told him that I wanted to get his opinion about a poem. A copy of the poem was first given to me by a principal at one of my schools, and over the years, I had encountered different versions of it in different learning environments. Although the author of the poem is unknown, I can't help but believe that it was written by someone like Johnny. I used to read the poem to the toughest, most troubled students.

Why I Can't Tell You Who I Am

Don't be fooled by me.
Don't be fooled by the face I wear.
For I wear a mask, I wear a thousand masks, masks I'm
afraid to take off, and none of them are me.
Pretending is an art that's second nature with me, but
don't be fooled.
For God's sake don't be fooled.
I give you the impression that I'm secure,
That all is sunny and unruffled with me, within as well as
without,
That confidence is my name and coolness my game.
But please don't believe me. Please!
My surface may seem smooth, but my surface is my mask.
Beneath dwells the real me in confusion, in fear, in
aloneness.
But I hide this.
I panic at the thought of my weakness and fear being
exposed.
To shield me from the glance that knows.
But such a glance is precisely my salvation.
My only salvation, and I know it.
That is, if it's followed by forgiveness, and acceptance,
If it's followed by love.

It's the only thing that can liberate me from myself,
From my own self-built prison walls.
It's the only thing that will assure me of what I can't
assure myself,
That I'm really worth something.
I'm afraid that deep down I'm nothing, that I'm just no
good,
And that you will see this and reject me.
Please listen carefully and try to hear what I'm NOT
saying.
I dislike hiding. Honestly.
You've got to hold out your hand even when that's the last
thing I seem to want, or need.
Please choose to.
It will not be easy for you.
Who am I, you may wonder? I am someone you know
very well.
For I am every man you meet. I am every woman.

As I read the poem, Johnny's eyes became teary, which he controlled by looking up, then looking away as though not interested. He sniffed. Then, with head held high, he said, "Well, so? That could be anyone." He left abruptly, likely because he was feeling emotions rise that he didn't want to feel. He was trying to save face.

A few phrases in the poem suggest the most effective strategy to use with a bully: "I panic at the thought of my weakness and fear being exposed" and "A glance that knows... is my salvation... if it's followed by forgiveness, acceptance,"... [and] love..." I kept appealing to Johnny's good qualities rather than his limitations. I now knew from his response to the poem, as I had suspected, that underneath his angry facade was vulnerability. After spending enough time with Johnny so that he knew I wasn't going to hurt him, I arranged a meeting with him and four other students in his class. He was going to be interviewed for a job the following week, and I told him that the purpose of our meeting was to put together a résumé. He had never heard of one, so I explained that it was like a report card that listed only his positive qualities. I told him that it would have none of the things on it that he was used to seeing, such as "I lose my temper all the time," "I never finish my work," or "I started a fire in the locker room and got suspended." Because he wanted the job, he cooperated without complaint. We discussed the job skills he already had and listed them on the résumé. Knowing that he was respected by others in his class, I asked them to come up with qualities they had observed in Johnny. They did so eagerly, and soon we had a long list of his positive qualities, the first of which was leadership.

Coincidentally, right after this session, as Johnny was walking back to class, another student ran out of a classroom in an angry explosion of temper. Three teachers ran after him. Johnny knew that if the student continued to run, there would be serious consequences. He called out, "Hey, chill, dude." Because Johnny's words were so powerful, the student stopped and listened to him, something no teacher was able to get to happen. "That's an example of your leadership," I told him, and Johnny was startled and pleased.

With a lot of help and patience from those at his school, Johnny was able to use the power behind his bullying to positively affect his life. After graduating from his continuation high school, he enrolled in the Job Corps for further skill training.

You go about your life with the intention to give love, to make a contribution, to do your best. Someone becomes angry and verbally abusive. How do you respond? Now you have several options to choose from. These techniques may sound foreign and difficult to use at first, but like skiing in our earlier example, using these tools becomes automatic with practice. I have tested all of them over the years, and I know how powerful they are. I hope you will test them yourself, and try to make them a part of your life. The tools described in this chapter will give you more confidence as you face the difficult people in your life. By establishing rapport, you earn their trust. By

setting boundaries, by standing up to them, or asking for what you want, you gain their respect. By keeping what you say loving, you defuse the conflict. By listening without judgment, you provide an arena for peace.

The exercises at the end of this chapter will help you to get started. Choose one of the following exercises to practice each day. At the end of the day, write in your notebook about your experience. Students who learn these strategies inevitably emerge from the experience with a quiet confidence. They know that they possess the knowledge that they can positively affect situations.

In the next, and last, chapter of this book, I will invite you to welcome the inevitability of death into your life. No lesson from any of the other chapters in this book carries as much significance as accepting that our time, and the time of those we love and those we encounter during our day, is limited.

~ ~

Exercise 1: Listening without Judgment

Today, listen without judging. If you find yourself judging, make a list of your judgments in your notebook and ask yourself (nonjudgmentally) how they apply to you.

Exercise 2: Asking Open-ended Questions

Today, instead of giving advice, find an opportunity to ask open-ended questions to help other people find their own answers. Instead of saying, "I think you should do X," ask, "What have you considered so far?" Instead of saying, "You shouldn't do X," ask, "What would be the result of choosing that?"

Exercise 3: Using Metaphors

Today, find an appropriate opportunity to relate an encouraging story to someone who is discouraged or stuck. For example, if someone feels like giving up, after listening to the person, you might share a tale of another who kept on going even when all appeared hopeless and who was rewarded with a better outcome.

Exercise 4: Spending Time with a Difficult Person

Today, as an experiment, take all the time needed with a difficult person. Let other things go, just for today, as if this experiment is the most important thing you could be doing.

Exercise 5: Using Support-Empathy-Truth Statements

Today, practice using S.E.T. statements with someone who is unable to hear another viewpoint. Your three-part statement will include your support of the individual. You will imagine how the person feels at the present moment and how you might feel and act similarly under the same circumstances, and you will put this understanding into words. You will tell the truth without fear.

For example, "I know you need those four reports. You must be feeling frustrated that I'm not finished yet. I will need at least another week to complete them all."

Exercise 6: Establishing Rapport

Today, mirror posture while talking with someone or while sitting silently.

Today, practice matching the vocal volume of someone else, speaking in approximately the same tone, pace, and volume as another.

Today, pace your breathing to another's by watching the person's shoulders or chest, and breathe in sync with the person.

Today, listen for auditory, visual, or kinesthetic preferences in another's speech. If you notice that one of these styles is predominant, match your choice of predicates with it.

Exercise 7: Standing Up to a Bully

To stand up to someone being hostile and aggressive, first remove any characterization of the person (such as "bully") and mirror the person's posture. If the person shouts, raise your vocal volume while keeping your attitude clear of your "stuff." Speak your truth. If you feel stress, accept responsibility for how you feel and set that aside for later.

8

DEATH: THE INVISIBLE RINGMASTER

Even throughout life, 'tis death that makes life live,
Gives it whatever the significance.

—Robert Browning, *The Ring and the Book*

Death is the mother of beauty.

—Wallace Stevens, "Sunday Morning"

The doors of death are ever open.

—Jeremy Taylor, *Contemplation on the State of Man*

The premeditation of death is the premeditation of liberty.
He who has learnt to die, has unlearnt to serve.

—Montaigne

Death tugs at my ear and says, "Live, I am coming."

—Oliver Wendell Holmes

*T*he lion tamer stepped into the cage with Tonga and five
other male African lions descended from a Serengeti pride. Now an
adult, raised in captivity since he was born, Tonga, like the others,
had spent most of the day lazing and sleeping. As a crowd of people began to fill the amphitheater, the animals grew restless. The
other lions took their places as practiced, but Tonga paced, then

164   LION TAMING

strutted with his tail lashing up and down. His mouth was slightly open, with his lips set in a straight line covering his teeth. A small boy in the crowd shouted, "Look, Mommy! The kitty is happy! He's wagging his tail and smiling."

Nothing could be further from the truth. Tonga was posturing, displaying a show of dominance in an effort to gain power. Perhaps it was from possessiveness; some cats grow so attached to their trainers that they don't like them even to look at other lions. Fear began to creep along the lion tamer's spine, signaling to her that control in the cage was shifting from her to the powerful, pacing animal. Tonga began to roar, and soon so did the others. She knew what could happen if the struggle for power escalated. Because lions work together to overcome prey of gazelle, antelope, or impala, she knew that if Tonga attacked her, the other lions likely would follow. She had to put a stop to the shift in power. So much could be lost if the lions seized control from her. Even if she could escape the cage unharmed, she could never again spend time safely with these lions because they would never again relinquish power to her.

Unlike most of us, lion tamers must risk their lives regularly. That is what lion tamers do. No one can step into a cage with several lions without first accepting the possibility that she could be killed by the animals. No lion tamer walks into such a situation without considerable training and time spent bonding with the lions. Despite their extensive preparation, however, lion tamers never lower their guard with the lions; they never forget that the animals are never truly tame and always pose a very real physical threat. You probably are not one of those who must, because of your choice of profession or because of illness, seriously and honestly look at death, but I recommend that you make the effort anyway because consideration of your own death can transform your personality in extremely positive ways. I don't mean a morbid, self-pitying consideration that leads to a withdrawal into the comfort zone, but an open, honest examination and acceptance of the fact that your time here is limited.

Many people who have nearly died—through accident, disease, or some other reason—come away from the experience with a greater capacity for living. They find themselves no longer burdened by the fears that constrict so many of us. I consider myself lucky to be in that group, and I'll describe my own experience later in this chapter. By overcoming your fear of death, you overcome the greatest and most paralyzing fear of them all. Interestingly, for most of us, that fear lies out of sight, beneath all the others. By acknowledging and releasing it, however, you'll find that your other fears drop away. And without the fear that interferes with our ability to connect with others, you will find that your relationships—even with those you once considered difficult—improve.

This chapter asks you to examine your relationship with death: How do thoughts of your own death and the deaths of those closest to you make you feel? Can you hold these thoughts in your mind, or does your discomfort lead you to shift your attention elsewhere? In Chapter 2, I stated that fear lies behind the anger of difficult people. In this chapter, we'll examine the greatest fear of all—the fear of death—and I'll present discussion and exercises to help you make peace with the idea of dying.

The Danger of Denial

In *Conversations at Midnight; Coming to Terms with Dying and Death*, a dying man wrote about how his anxieties about death were soothed when he shared them with his wife, Kay:

> *The life story of every human being is a variation on the theme of loss through death—of every pet, every friend, every loved one, until, sooner or later, the self, too, is taken. Yet this familiar companion on our journey remains a feared and hostile presence until the end; a dark assassin who waits in shadows until he cuts down. Yet since there is no escaping death's company, doesn't it make sense to call it out of the shadows and make its acquaintance? This is the task that lies before Kay and me.*[1]

The writer's call for an open acknowledgment of death is healthy. Unfortunately, it's also rare. Denial is the American way of responding to the issue of death.

Our lives are filled with endings. Some we experience daily. An evening of sleep ends, and a day of work begins. The work day is over, a meal is consumed, the waking part of the day is over, and again it's time to sleep. Then the time to sleep is over, and we wake up to repeat the process. We do not grieve such a frequently repeated pattern. Other endings are less familiar and cause us discomfort: Our babies become teenagers (good grief!), our pets die, our youth fades. Some of the hardest endings are those turning points in our lives that arrive with a complex combination of emotions: We feel a mixture of gladness and sadness when a child leaves the nest, the feelings of liberation that accompany a divorce are followed by the unpleasant discovery that our inner critic happily steps in to take the role once filled by a difficult spouse, and retirement arrives with a combination of relief and grief.

Despite the daily reminders to the contrary, we deny that the process is natural. Instead of acknowledging and accepting the endings in our lives, we run from them by keeping ourselves busy or masking them with mind-numbing substances. We hide from these feelings, when accepting them is what makes them heal. Most of us seem to sense at a subconscious level that endings are inherently bad and to be avoided if possible. Often, even when something we want to end reaches its conclusion, we still feel sadness and perhaps some confusion at these feelings. It's not the ending that we fear, however, but the unknown that yawns open before us in the space once occupied by something familiar. And no ending fills us with as much fear as death.

Death is a comparatively rare visitor to our lives, partly because our society has become so fragmented and our circle of close family members and friends is smaller than it was for previous generations. Our youth-oriented culture discourages from everyday living discussion of aging and death, creating an unnatural silence around an issue that cannot be denied for long. This denial of what is inevitable forces that energy to erupt in fears and anxieties. Professor of Psychiatry

J. E. Meyer, M.D., claims in *Death and Neurosis* that denied fears of death that are not allowed avenues of expression become ways people cope (defense strategies).[2] Because the tendency is to deny thinking about death, he says, phobias, obsessive neuroses, hypochondriasis (overconcern for one's physical health), and addictions become the avenues for expression. Thus, agoraphobia, or fear of being in open or public places, originates as a fear of death. Claustrophobia and fear of the dark are other equivalents of the fear of death.

Our anxiety about death provides us with a sense that something is wrong, and we look to the external world to find "causes." The experience manifests in many ways. Some symptoms of fear of death include the following:

* a feeling of running out of time
* feeling pressured from having too much to do
* fear of not having enough money
* dread of aging
* fear of going out in public
* fear of closed-in places
* fear of the dark
* fear of pain and suffering
* fear of missing out
* fear of making a mistake
* fear of being alone
* fear of looking foolish
* fear of rejection

Whether you are in a state of fear because you are dealing with a difficult person, or an angry person is expressing his fear with rage, if you traced either of these feelings back to their origins, you would discover a fear of death. The fear isn't irrational because we all will die, but it isn't necessarily conscious in our minds. Fear erupts because it is unconsciously present within us, and we do not allow it a presence in our lives. In my work, I sometimes become intimate with people's deepest selves, and those willing to look deep within themselves find their fear of death waiting in the darkness.

Norma, a divorced woman approaching sixty, spoke in one of my classes about being alone and feeling lonely. She wanted a close relationship with a man. To get at the fear underlying her concerns, we asked her open-ended questions. Then we staged her worst-case scenario in a psychodrama. At times, the person presenting the issue takes a role in the drama. At other times, he or she watches as others in class take on the situations described for them. Norma chose to observe four others play out her concern. Standing outside of the drama, Norma realized that she believed that she would be unhappy if she were not in a relationship. As she traced her fear back, she moved from "I'm getting old, and I'm afraid I'll be alone all the time, and I'll be so lonely that no one will talk to me" to "If I'm lonely all the time, I'll be so unhappy that no one will want to be around me" to "I'll lose my job because I'll act so strangely. Then I'll be eating out of garbage cans. Then I'll die alone." She didn't really believe that she would eat out of garbage cans when she spoke about it in class, but the presence of her unexpressed fear led her to sense impending doom.

In another case, a twenty-five-year-old woman told us that she had seldom spoken during the previous nineteen years. After describing incidents of childhood abuse by an older cousin, she felt fear from the disclosure even though the cousin had long since moved to another state. She said, "It feels like I'll die." It took several weeks to get at the fears behind the problem. She kept it a secret all those years, thinking that if she did otherwise she would die.

A man in one of my classes who could not stand up to his verbally hostile boss told us, "He'll fire me." Then he added, "I won't be able to find another job. I won't have any money. I'll be ashamed. I'll lose my house because I won't be able to make the payments. I'll have to live in a shelter. I'll start drinking..."

The final fear, fear of death, if not allowed expression, transforms itself into various forms of fears and anxieties. In childhood, it is seen in fear of the dark or fear of separation from a parent. When we become adults, it manifests as fear of failure, fear of succeeding, and so on. In severe cases, it becomes generalized fear and manifests in crippling emotional conditions that leave the individual free to avoid living actively in the world. The fear is an exaggeration of reality, and the process of uncovering it releases the individual from its grasp. Time after time, in my classes, I have seen these fears lose their hold over the individuals after they are expressed. Afterward, the class participants go about their lives with renewed clarity and vitality.

Allowing Death a Place in Your Heart

Lion tamers don't spend a lot of time fearing their own death around the animals. They've chosen to spend lots of time with them. There is always a healthy respect, however, that comes from understanding the nature of the beasts. Accepting death creates a paradox: By allowing its presence a space in her life, the lion tamer no longer fears it. The fear is the result of pushing it away. Once invited in, it becomes a helpful ally, keeping her alert and appreciative of her life.

When you face and take into your heart the fact that our bodies die, you can fully appreciate the current moments and the people who are close to you. And knowing that death also awaits the difficult person before you, you are more likely to feel compassion than fear when dealing with him.

We allow death a place in our lives by applying the healing process described in Chapter 5 to the concept of death. By permitting ourselves to own all parts of ourselves and release suppressed negative emotions on an ongoing basis, we will find our feelings about death. By acknowledging how we do feel and accepting it, we return to our natural state of peace. To accept death, think of it, take it into your heart—that is, visualize your thought about death as moving to your heart area— and let it be there. You might have one or more of several different feelings about death: "I accept that I hate that I will die" or "I think the end is the end—nothingness" or "I believe the ending of this life marks the beginning of another, but I don't know what to expect." Or, "It's OK that I will die, but I hate to think that [name of person] will die" or "It's not dying that bothers me; it's [growing old, suffering, looking back with regret at a life unlived].'' Accept however you feel about it, and reap the benefits of this acceptance.

The fear of death yields to feelings of love and peace when we take death into our heart as part of our life. The inevitability of death unites us all and serves as a reminder of what's really important. In difficult situations, if you remember the connectedness of us all, then you are in a better position to extend love. Sometimes, extending love takes the form of setting a boundary or saying no with a lightness that comes from "having the big picture" in mind. Or if you perceive the difficult person as a mirror of your own disowned pain, you might know that your physical response signals your own call for healing something internal. You might view this other person as a part of yourself calling out for help.

By remembering that we all die, we become able to include the idea of death in our lives, even with all its attendant grief and pain. It becomes an excellent advisor for making conscious choices about your life. Nothing is more helpful to you in determining your life's priorities, as I discovered during a harrowing visit to the hospital.

An Encounter with Death

Almost twenty years ago, I had an encounter with death in the hospital following two operations. My body ached from surgical stitches and fever. I felt alone; more alone than I'd ever felt even though I had a steady stream of visitors. I knew that my estranged husband would not be calling because we had recently decided to separate, and we were too ashamed to announce the news of our failed marriage. I missed my youngest daughter's first steps and the sight of my five-year-old running wild. My once-healthy body weighed less than 100 pounds, and I was running high fevers and suffering from adhesions caused by gangrene. Large doses of antibiotics and two surgeries had not alleviated the problem.

Remembering a scene from only two weeks before sent me into despair: I had written my husband a note filled with my blaming anger. I wished that everything could be all right again between us, but I knew it could not. Beside my bed stood a nightstand supporting a telephone, a plain box of tissue, and a water glass. I turned my head to look at the telephone as if I could energize it into ringing. Perhaps the loneliness I felt made me long for communication. I wanted my estranged husband to call and say that my health would return and that our relationship would be transformed magically to one of living happily ever after, revealing the appearance of the lack of love between us as a bad dream.

My health sank to a low point in the middle of the night, and I experienced the following waking "dream": A shaft of light descended from an upper corner of the room, slanting down to my bed and enveloping me. "Oh!" I said, startled. Just as I had read in accounts of similar experiences, I felt all my cares, regrets, and longings drop away. Before, I had worried about the grades I would earn in graduate school, my failed marriage and the stigma of divorce, my inability to do a good job raising my children, the jealousy my oldest daughter felt toward her sister, what my husband's family would think of our separation, how I would raise two small children as a single parent, how to get rid of the pain in my body— the list was endless. Instead, at this moment, my body felt free, light, without a trace of discomfort. I felt myself leave my ailing body on the bed. A soft humming guided me halfway down the corridor of light where the warmth enveloped me with intense bliss. Smiling, a guide in white robes embraced me. He resembled Mahatma Guru Charanand, a man from India I heard speak once before. "You see?" he questioned, without saying a word.

Those two "words" contained more wisdom than an entire library. They made perfect sense to me then. None of it mattered: the unfairness of the world, the crime, the hate, the victimization of innocent children and elderly citizens. I could never fully describe the sense of peace that enveloped me. Fill your mind completely with the thought of your own death—all the people you would never see again and the experiences you would never have again—and then bring your full attention to this moment, this precious, unique moment, knowing that you are still alive, that your loved ones are still here. If you can imagine that peaceful feeling magnified one hundred times, then you can begin to experience how that moment felt to me.

I was ready to go forward through the corridor. While in my body, I would not have wanted to abandon my children by dying, but in the tunnel I had no such cares. The wordless "you see" seemed to explain all suffering so clearly, and yet I can't capture in words the feeling of that experience. The closest I can come is this childhood song:

> Row, row, row your boat
> gently down the stream.
> Merrily, merrily, merrily, merrily
> life is but a dream.

The song tells us that life is only a dream, and when it is sung in a round by groups of children, with the different layers of voices, the repetition of terms, and the perpetually cycling lyrics, it appropriately takes on a somewhat surreal, disorienting, dreamlike quality of its own. In the tunnel, I came to understand that life is a waking dream against a backdrop of infinity, and I welcomed the thought that my life on earth was now over. But then my eyes locked with the eyes of the robed guide, and in that moment I knew I had to return. There was more, much more for me to do. Reluctantly, I went back to my body and the pain.

What did I take from my visit to the tunnel? The simple knowledge that we all manifest from the same energy. When one of us dies, another is born, and when another dies, another gives birth. The invisible energy that I spoke about in Chapter 1 is out there for us if we want to tap into it. It is also within us. It is what we are made of. Although we are all "cells" of that energy, we get lost in the drama of our lives here on earth because life here is so filled with distractions. The understanding conveyed to me in the "dream" made me feel a lightness that I had not felt before. I realized that although each of us chooses a certain role in life, fundamentally, we are all part of the same energy. Ultimately, we are each other.

Death as Coach

Most of us, even those who believe that consciousness or a soul lives on after the death of our bodies, seem to perceive death negatively. What seems to make it frightening is that thoughts of death force us to acknowledge our feelings of having unfinished business, of not being authentic (a life unlived), of missing our opportunity to make a contribution, of thwarted intentions, of the fear of pain, and of the fear of dying alone, unloved. I recommend holding an entirely different image of death in your mind. Instead of imagining a grim reaper poised to cut you and your loved ones down and separate you from the joys of your life, imagine death as a coach, a friend who will tell you the truth when you need to be reminded to make the most of your time here because your stay is short.

I don't know exactly what my spiritual experience in the hospital meant. The result of it, however, was an urgency to learn everything I could about raising kids, to finish graduate school, to make peace with my husband even as we finalized our divorce, and to begin to make my contribution. It left me with the realization that every moment matters. When I gave death an important position in my life, it became my best teacher.

By allowing death to remind you of the "big picture," you have a coach, an encouraging advisor, to bring you back to a larger consciousness when you focus too much on trivial details, such as landing that promotion, competing for top positions, and struggling with difficult people. When you struggle with a difficult person, you and the other person are stuck in fear. The fear shows itself as some kind of miscommunication or a struggle for power. When you have death as your coach, you will always be able to step back and view a larger perspective. Instead of feeling angry, frustrated, or hopeless, you feel compassion and love. From that place, you figure out what the best action is. You live and breathe and move in an expanded comfort zone. You are comfortable inside, so wherever you go and whatever you say, there is peace.

When I'm interacting with a difficult person, I imagine that this day is the last for one of us. I wonder, "What will I say, now that it's this man's (or woman's) last day on earth?," or "What can I say if this is my last meeting?" All considerations of politics or reputation fall away. When someone is irritable or hostile, you can entertain such questions as "What fear lies behind this anger?" and perceive it as fear needing love, sometimes in the form of taking a stand. Silently, you can ask yourself, "What in my heart do I really want to say to this person?" When you consult death as your coach in these matters, you are able to speak your truth without the attitude. That is to say, you are not trying to win or to be right; you are only being real. These considerations get you clear of your "stuff" and in a position to help.

With death as your coach, you can make daily choices in your life to ensure a life well-lived. This means something different to each of us and may mean departing from what "mainstream" society views as important. I know one secretary who, after returning from a funeral, decided to express to people in her life how much they meant to her. She made telephone calls and sent notes and verbalized her love and caring thoughts to each significant person in her life. A manager of an engineering company told an employee that he appeared very depressed and recommended that he seek counseling, an area rarely mentioned in the corporate world. A married couple who had planned separate vacations gave away one trip to a friend and went together to Hawaii. A music teacher left education and opened up her own business doing colors and make-up. A lawyer left his field to become a high school math teacher. A famous opera singer left music to try her hand at business. An office manager joined a choir and enrolled in voice lessons. A childless rancher and his wife adopted two children whose mother had died of AIDS. No one but you can know what is in your heart wanting expression. No one but you can get it to happen. Find what makes your heart quicken with excitement.

~⊰ ⊱~

Coach Death helps with all the elements of dealing with difficult people that I have addressed in this book: It supports you as you stretch the boundaries of your comfort zone, increase your willingness to take risks, and state your truth. In the area of characterization, the acknowledgment of death reminds you to remove your judgments in your dealings with others. It is the perfect teacher who gently reminds you to take the time to heal your inner self by turning up the volume on this moment. You are your attention. How much of your attention can you bring to the present? To keep in mind, as Dan Millman said, that "there are no ordinary moments,"³ ask yourself, "If I knew that this person being difficult were going to die tomorrow, what would I say right now?"

Death is the invisible ringmaster. It controls our actions and thoughts, and usually we're not even aware of it. But we can gain control, paradoxically, by admitting that we have no control, by acknowledging that death cannot be denied and then acting accordingly. The world needs you to accept the responsibility for your life and how you feel about it. The world needs you to be your unique self. Our society is hurting. Our children crave love, peace, and a sense of belonging, and in their desperation to obtain these things in a world less and less capable of providing them, they attempt to find them through drugs, crime, and involvement with gangs. People of all ages suffer unnecessarily and add to each other's pain, not understanding the remarkable power they possess to transform their lives and the lives of everyone around them. Be a warrior for peace, and as you heal yourself, you will heal those around you, and they will do the same, creating a gentle wave of healing that expands far beyond ourselves, and together we can look forward to a future of greater peace and understanding.

~⊰ ⊱~

Exercise 1: Death as Coach

Recognizing the powerful positive effect that accepting death as your coach can have on your life, ask yourself the following questions regularly to monitor your relationships with others:

- ❧ Imagine that you have just attended the funeral of a friend. Spending time alone afterward, what thoughts might you have about your own life? Is there someone you've been meaning to see? Is there a trip you've been meaning to take? Is there work to be done? Is there something to create?
- ❧ To whom would you want to communicate unexpressed love?
- ❧ Whom would you want to forgive?
- ❧ To whom would you need to make amends?
- ❧ If you knew this would be the last time you saw [name of a difficult person], what would you want to say to him or her right now?

Exercise 2: Living Every Day as if It Were Your Last

This exercise is to be done for thirty days. Mark the first and last of the thirty days on your calendar. Use the following thoughts to guide you each day:

- ❧ I will not wait to tell those I meet how much I appreciate them.
- ❧ I will send a card or letter to someone who is lonely.
- ❧ I will be peacefully truthful to a person I have thought of as difficult.
- ❧ I will finish any unfinished business by forgiving someone.
- ❧ I take responsibility for my thoughts and feelings and how they create my mood.
- ❧ I am living today as if it is my last day.

LION TAMING PROCESS

Am I stretching my comfort zone?

Invisible spirit

Do I realize that I'm bigger than my thoughts?
Do I realize that (name of a difficult person) is bigger than
whatever he or she is stuck in right now?
Am I characterizing?
Have I spent some time imagining an ideal outcome?

My "Stuff" mind

How much is my own physiology going off?
Is there something being mirrored for me to heal?

Doing body

How much of my truth is it safe to deliver?
Am I remembering the components of rapport?
- *Mirroring posture*
- *Matching predicates*

Listening

- *Am I really present for this person, or am I trying to change them?*
- *Is there an open-ended question I can ask?*

Coach Death

What would I say if I knew one or the other of us were going to die tomorrow?

The world needs me to be who I am.

NOTES

Chapter One: The Invisible Realm

1 Thomas F. Crum, *The Magic of Conflict: Turning a Life of Work into a Work of Art* (New York: Simon & Schuster, Inc., 1987), 41.

2 Ibid., 89.

3 David D. Burns, M.D., *Feeling Good: The New Mood Therapy* (New York: Signet, 1981).

4 Viktor E. Frankl, *Man's Search for Meaning*, rev. ed. (New York: Washington Square Press, 1984), 12.

5 Thank you to Louis Baum, Sr., director of the Sacramento Attitudinal Healing Center, for introducing me to this idea.

Chapter Three: Removing the Mask of the Lion

1 Faces of the Enemy: Reflections of the Hostile Imagination by Sam Keen. © 1986 by Sam Keen. Reprinted by permission of HarperCollins Publishers, Inc.

2 Thank you to Maria Nemeth, of Maria Nemeth Ph.D. & Associates, for this idea.

Chapter Five: Healing the Inner Lion

1 Claudio is a Chilean chef and a dear friend of my family.

2 This quote from Carl G. Jung from a radio broadcast appears in the transcript "The Fight with the Shadow," *Listener*, November 7, 1946.

3 *A Course in Miracles®*, Volume One, Text, 328. © 1975. Reprinted by permission of the Foundation for Inner Peace, Inc., P.O. box 598, Mill Valley, CA 94942.

4 Ibid., 329.

5 Reprinted with permission of Stan Wells. © 1973 by Stan Wells.

6 Susan Trout, *To See Differently: Personal Growth and Being of Service through Attitudinal Healing* (Washington, D.C.: Three Roses Press, 1990), 48-51.

7 Barbara Hannah, *Encounters with the Soul: Active Imagination as Developed by C.G. Jung* (Boxton Sigo Press, 1981), 7.

8 Fahizah Alim, "The Miracle of Joan Fountain," *The Sacramento Bee*, January 11, 1994, C1.

Chapter Six: Satisfying the Inner Lion

1 *Times Alone: Selected Poems of Antonio Machado*, (Wesleyan University Press, 1983). Translated by Robert Bly. Reprinted by permission of Robert Bly.

2 Wayne W. Dyer, *Gifts from Eykis* (New York: Simon & Schuster, 1983).

Chapter Seven: Tools of the Trade

1 Churchill spoke these words in a speech about the war effort in a radio broadcast addressed to President Franklin Roosevelt on February 9, 1941.

2 Adapted from "A Kind Word Turneth Away Wrath", by Terry Dobson, printed in *Aikido and the New Warrior*, edited by Richard Strozzi Heckler. (North Atlantic Books, Berkeley, California), 1985. Used by permission of the publisher.

3 Jerold J. Kreisman, M.D., and Hal Straus, *I Hate You—Don't Leave Me: Understanding the Borderline Personality* (New York: Avon Books, 1991).

Chapter Eight: Death: The Invisible Ringmaster

1 Herbert and Kay Kramer, *Conversations at Midnight: Coming to Terms with Dying and Death* (New York: William Morrow and Company, 1993), 30.

2 Joachim E. Meyer, M.D., *Death and Neurosis*, (New York: New York International Universities Press, Inc., 1975).

3 Dan Millman, *Way of the Peaceful Warrior: A Book That Changes Lives*, (Tiburon, H J Kramer, Inc., 1984).

BIBLIOGRAPHY

Abrams, Jeremiah, and Connie Zweig, eds. *Meeting the Shadow: The Hidden Power of the Dark Side of Human Nature*. Los Angeles: Jeremy P. Tarcher, Inc., 1991.

A Course in Miracles. Tiburon: Foundation for Inner Peace, 1975.

Alim, Fahizah. "The Miracle of Joan Fountain," *The Sacramento Bee*, January 11, 1994, C1.

Burns, David D., M.D. *Feeling Good: The New Mood Therapy*. New York: Signet, 1981.

Chopra, Deepak, M.D. *Ageless Body, Timeless Mind: The Quantum Alternative to Growing Old*. New York: Harmony Books, 1993.

Crum, Thomas F. *The Magic of Conflict: Turning a Life of Work into a Work of Art*. New York: Simon & Schuster, Inc., 1987.

Dass, Ram, and Paul Gorman. *How Can I Help? Stories and Reflections on Service*. New York: Alfred A. Knopf, Inc., 1985.

Dobson, Terry. "A Kind Word Turneth Away Wrath," printed in *Aikido* and the *New Warrior*, edited by Richard Strozzi Heckler. Berkeley: North Atlantic Books, 1985.

Dyer, Wayne W., Dr. *Gifts from Eykis*. New York: Simon & Schuster, 1983.

Frankl, Viktor E. *Man's Search for Meaning*, rev. ed. New York: Washington Square Press, 1984.

Hannah, Barbara. *Encounters with the Soul: Active Imagination as Developed by C.G. Jung*. Sigo Press, Boston, 1981.

Jampolsky, Gerald G., M.D. *Love Is Letting Go of Fear*. Berkeley: Bantam Books, 1981.

Kramer, Herbert and Kay. *Conversations at Midnight: Coming to Terms with Dying and Death*. New York: William Morrow and Company, 1993.

Kreisman, Jerold J., M.D., and Hal Straus. *I Hate You—Don't Leave Me: Understanding the Borderline Personality*. New York: Avon Books, 1991.

McWilliams, Peter. *Do It! Let's Get Off Our Buts*. Los Angeles: Prelude Press, 1991.

Meyer, Joachim E., M.D. *Death and Neurosis*. Translated by Margarete Nunberg. New York: New York International Universities Press, Inc., 1975.

Millman, Dan. *Way of the Peaceful Warrior: A Book That Changes Lives*. Tiburon: H J Kramer, Inc., 1984.

Ryan, M. J., ed. *A Grateful Heart: Daily Blessings for the Evening Meal from Buddha to the Beatles*. Berkeley: Conari Press, 1994.

Shaughnessy, Susan. *Walking on Alligators: A Book of Meditations for Writers*. New York: HarperSanFrancisco, 1993.

Trout, Susan. *To See Differently: Personal Growth and Being of Service through Attitudinal Healing*. Washington, D.C.: Three Roses Press, 1990.

FURTHER READING

Andrews, Lewis M., Ph.D. *To Thine Own Self Be True: The Relationship between Spiritual Values and Emotional Health*. New York: Doubleday, 1989.

Besant, Annie, and C. W. Leadbeater. *Thought-forms*. London: The Theosophical Publishing House, 1925.

Cameron, Charles, and Suzanne Elusorr. T.G.I.M.: "Thank God It's Monday," *Making Your Work Fulfilling and Finding Fulfilling Work*. Los Angeles: Jeremy P. Tarcher, Inc., 1986.

Carter, Jay. *Nasty People: How to Stop Being Hurt by Them without Becoming One of Them*. Chicago: Contemporary Books, 1989.

Estes, Clarissa Pinkola, Ph.D. *Women Who Run with the Wolves: Myths and Stories of the Wild Woman Archetype*. New York: Ballantine Books, 1992.

Fox, Emmet. *Around the Year with Emmet Fox: A Book of Daily Readings*. San Francisco: Harper & Row, 1958.

Hendricks, Harville, Dr. *Getting the Love You Want: A Guide for Couples*. New York: Harper & Row, 1988.

Jeffers, Susan, Ph.D. *Feel the Fear and Do It Anyway*. New York: Fawcett Columbine, 1987.

Johnson, Robert A. *Owning Your Own Shadow: Understanding the Dark Side of the Psyche*. New York: HarperSanFrancisco, 1991.

Marrs, Donald. *Executive in Passage: Career in Crisis—The Door to Uncommon Fulfillment*. Los Angeles: Barrington Sky Publishing, 1990.

McWilliams, Peter. *You Can't Afford the Luxury of a Negative Thought: A Book for People with Any Life-Threatening Illness— Including Life*. Los Angeles: Prelude Press, 1989.

Meade, Michael. *Men and the Water of Life: Initiation and the Tempering of Men*. New York: Harper San Francisco, 1993.

Paulus, Trina. *Hope for the Flowers*. Mahwah, N.J.: Paulist Press, 1972.

Sinetar, Marsha. *Do What You Love, the Money Will Follow: Discovering Your Right Livelihood*. New York: Dell Publishing, 1987.

Williamson, Marianne. *A Return to Love: Reflections on the Principles of A Course in Miracles*. New York: Harper Perennial, 1993.

INDEX

ABOUT THE AUTHOR

*B*etty Perkins, who earned an M.S. in educational counseling with a credential in school psychology, is a Neurolinguistic Programmer Practitioner and trained mediator. She has worked as a school psychologist for twelve years and teaches a graduate course in human interaction at the University of LaVerne School of Continuing Education in Fair Oaks, California. For years, she has given workshops, speeches, and seminars addressing the topic of dealing with difficult people to administrators, counselors, therapists, and the small business community.